DON'T MESS WITH T'AMNA

A Novel Inspired by Real Events

By Jim Shon

The Kwan-dok-jong in Cheju City

DON'T MESS WITH T'AMNA
A Novel Inspired by Real Events
Copyright © 2024 Jim Shon

All rights reserved. No part of this book may be used or reproduced by any means, graphic, electronic, or mechanical, including photocopying, recording, taping or by any information storage retrieval system without the written permission of the author except in the case of brief quotations embodied in critical articles and reviews.

The views expressed in this work are solely those of the author and do not necessarily reflect the views of the publisher, and the publisher hereby disclaims any responsibility for them. No warranties or guarantees are expressed or implied by the publisher's choice to include any of the content in this volume.

Neither the publisher nor the individual author(s) shall be liable for any physical, psychological, emotional, financial, or commercial damages, including, but not limited to, special, incidental, consequential or other damages. Our views and rights are the same: You are responsible for your own choices, actions, and results.

Because of the dynamic nature of the Internet, any web addresses or links contained in this book may have changed since publication and may no longer be valid.

Paperback:	9781733833189
eBook:	9781733833196

HAWAII
INSIGHT
BOOKS

HONOLULU, HI 96822
United States

Author's Comments

Don't Mess With T'amna – A Jeju Island Story, is a work of fiction inspired by real historical and current events. Hopefully, it is intriguing, educational, and entertaining. Names of characters have been mixed and matched with people I've known or real historical figures. None of this implies any attempt to comment on real people. Several are named after the Korean names given former Peace Corps Volunteers, but are not intended to be them. Occasionally, thinly devised organizational titles have been changed to respect their origins. The reader who knows about Cheju Island or Korean history will find genuine places, streets, and events that are well documented as true. There is a lot of older and newer history woven into the story. Excerpts from my personal journal are authentic.

Cheju is a real island, 90 miles off the southern coast of the Korean peninsula where I lived for three and a half years during a Peace Corps stint. A similar character hints at but does not represent my experience. Udo is a real island off the main island's eastern coast. The Kwan-dok-jong is a real 15th century pavilion smack in the middle of Cheju City. Seven-Star Street and the East Gate Market and Sarabong Hill and Mt. Halla are real. Those who served at the same time may find elements of the story familiar in the hope they will appreciate the inside origin of events they may have shared. I still have long standing friendships among Americans and Cheju residents who impacted my life fifty years ago. I think of Cheju as my second home, after where I was born in Syracuse NY, and my third and final home here in Hawaii, where I have happily lived most of my life.

T'amna, pronounced with a strong T, was indeed an original ancient name for Cheju. References to ancient rebellions and conflicts are accurate.

Amsterdam is a setting for part of the story, and most of the places are completely fictional. The political system of the Netherlands and Amsterdam is complicated. I have taken a fair amount of poetic license in setting events there. I did visit there once, briefly.

Each short chapter is written with a bit of a cinematic approach. Dialogue is central. As if you were watching a movie.

Amsterdam is a setting for part of the story, and most of the places are completely fictional. The political system of the Netherlands and Amsterdam is complicated. I have taken a fair amount of poetic license in setting events there. I did visit there once, briefly.

Each short chapter is written with a bit of a cinematic approach. Dialogue is central. As if you were watching a movie.

For spelling Korean names and places I've opted to use an old McCune Reischauer Romanization English system because it is far more accurate to the English ear and eye than the current system that softens most consonants and has other drawbacks. Thus, today's "Jeju" becomes "Cheju."

The author is grateful for the friendship, insights, and knowledge of colleagues during his Peace Corps service on Cheju, other members of the K-12 Korea group, especially those who served at the same time on Cheju, other RPCVs, and a special appreciation for those RPCVs whose initial brainstorming formed the basis of the story, particularly Dr. Bob and Kyung Swartout.

Much Aloha and Mahalo to former K-12 Karen Kushner, Esq., who edited the manuscript and made many suggested improvements.

Respect and gratitude to my Korean history professors at the University of Hawaii that allowed me to craft a multi-disciplinary thesis in the 1970s: Decision Making in Pre-Modern Korea.

Peace Corps on Jeju – 70 students in each class!

A Few Main Characters

Dr. Ahn No-oon, A Korean Scholar
Emily DeGroot, an Amsterdam politician
William Henry Hamilton, III
Eiko Hamilton, his wife
Masato Hamilton, his son
Hong Dae-shik, an attorney for the Sarabong Gang
Hyun P'il-song, A Prominent member of the Sarabong Gang kye promoting casinos
Inspector Bakker, an Amsterdam Police investigator
K.C. Sohn, a reporter
Dr. Kang Ki-sook, "Winston"- A Cheju Historian
Prof. Kim Ki-won, a former English Supervisor
Lee Yong- ho, A Vice Governor of Cheju
Ko Tae-jung, A Cheju activist
Ku Ga-yun, an attorney
Pu Kyung-ok, a Cheju activist
Suh Duk-hee, A young Cheju government translator
Yoo Chung-hee, A Judge
William van der Berg, Current Mayor of Amsterdam

PROLOGUE

It is a frenzied time of land and casino development and on the small island of Cheju (now spelled Jeju) the ancient Independent Kingdom of T'amna. Just off the coast of the Korean mainland it is now a tourist mecca. At the center of Jeju City a new casino is planned next to a 500-year-old Choson Dynasty Pavilion – the Kwandokjon – National Treasure #322.

Local activists with deep roots in Jeju's history launch a scheme to resist the development. A Korean American reporter is sent to Jeju, where he uncovers complex court cases seeking to wrestle back control of Jeju's history and its national treasures.

Find out how the near colonization of Korea in the 13th century by the Mongols, the shipwreck of Dutch traders in the 16th century, and the confiscation of property during the Japanese occupation impact protection of lands in modern times in the struggle to save Jeju's heritage.

A former American Peace Corps Volunteer living in Amsterdam attempts to track down ancient Dutch documents. Follow how a DNA ancestry test upsets casino schemes. Follow local gangs and shady-criminal developers and a surprising kidnapping. Appreciate the emergence two strong women leaders: a talented young female attorney, and the leadership of a Jeju woman activist to find out if they succeed. All set on the beautiful Island of Jeju, whose people have endured so much over the centuries, and who time and time again have stood up for their rights, and sent the message:

Don't Mess With T'amna - a Jeju Island Story

The characters and story were inspired by real events.

Chapter 1. Responsibility

Pu Kyung-ok leafed through her scrapbook, a ritual on the anniversary of her grandfather's passing. She could still hear his voice, giving her once again the *You Have A Responsibility talk*.

"Our family is one of the three original clans on the Island – Ko, Yang, and Pu. You may think this is a silly story, but we are respected, and expected to be leaders. Our ancestors were village heads, and some rose in the ranks of island wide government posts. You also come from a family of diving women, who, as you know, often were the main breadwinners of coastal villages."

"OK, grandfather, but what does that have to do with me?"

"Our family was not blessed with sons who survived the war, or who are living today. You, Kyung-ok, must step up and do your best for our clan, and our island."

His pictures had a theme. So many were taken in front of the ancient Yi Dynasty pavilion – the Kwan-dok-jong, located in the very center of the city. Endless high school and college graduation pictures, government and private ceremonies of all kinds, massive crowds in front of it for the Five-Day Open Markets. She had asked him about this.

"There are so many special places on this island. Mount Halla, Sunrise Hill, wonderful beaches. But the spiritual, political, and cultural soul has for hundreds of years been right here in Cheju City, the hub of all respectable events, the Kwang Dok Jong. Respect our history. Respect our heritage. Respect our culture. The Japanese burned down countless of our historical buildings, but thank goodness, for whatever reason, they left this one alone. We refurbished it. We repainted it. We preserved it for your generation. Keep it alive. Respect it. Know that buildings like this hold a special place in the hearts and minds of every child and family of Cheju."

Those conversations that she remembered had an impact on a young child of Cheju. She loved history, and she loved that special sense of responsibility.

Chapter 2. Curious Roots

Bill Hamilton sat staring at his packet of information from Descendents.com, the go-to website corporation where you could buy research on your roots. Much of the information he had already heard a bit from his family when young. *Hah, I'm ready to retire and I never took the time to look into my family's past,* he thought.

His full name was William Henry Hamilton, III. He was interested to learn that his great, great uncle wasn't a Henry but a Henrik, a common Dutch name. This is in part why he was happy to take the Descendants packet with him to Europe and accept the position in his insurance firm in London, and then a branch assignment in Amsterdam.

To be honest, he thought, *I'm a bit tired, dealing with deductibles, premiums, exemptions, rates, longevity charts, blah blah blah. Maybe it's time to bail out of this and retire.*

He was not surprised to learn that he had some Dutch DNA. But what was a puzzle was that he was also 1/16th Korean, and 1/32 Mongolian!!! "You've got to be kidding," he said out loud to himself. And the search for more distant relatives went cold when they could find no current references on various websites for Hamiltons connected to his family.

How astounding that he had served as a Peace Corps Volunteer on Korea's Cheju Island for over 3 years, and never knew. His mom was one eighth Japanese American from Hilo, Hawaii, and he had inherited only a slight hint of a non-European complexion. Of course, he blended in well growing up on Oahu, where so many of his classmates were of mixed ancestry.

"Hey Ted, you'll never believe this, but I actually have some Korean DNA!" he emailed his friend and fellow former Peace Corps buddy still living in Hawaii. They served on Cheju together, and were also fellow students in the University of Hawaii's History Department after Peace Corps. Bill was so into Korean history at the time, and wrote a very long, very eclectic, very multidisciplinary MA treatise on premodern Korea, that the traditionalist history profs totally rejected. So, he moved on and got an MBA and ended up with a career in international insurance.

"Bill, you are getting old. What, almost 72? Retire already. Stop living in the past. Let the Korean thing go. Take a cruise or something. Tell your wife Eiko we want to see you guys soon back here in Hawaii," he emailed back.

"Eiko, Ted thinks I should retire and move back home, maybe back to Hilo. What do you think?"

"Sweetie you never listen. I've been telling you that for the last three years. But it takes your PC buddy Ted to penetrate your stubborn skull. Before you pack, don't forget tomorrow is garbage and recycling day."

Hamilton's Japanese-American wife of 42 years was a professional in her own right; a long time senior research consultant for libraries looking into Japanese historical sources. Her fluency in the language, including the Kanji characters that were so much a part of East Asian records, made her a valuable asset in pouring through older records. At one time she was an expert witness in an international dispute over traditional navigation issues between Japan and Korea. She was glad she was mostly retired, but on occasion took a small contract job in Europe to keep her busy until she persuaded her husband to completely retire and head on back to Hawaii.

Bill wondered, if they did return to Hawaii, how his son Masato would react to having his nosy dad looking over his shoulder as he pursued his career in the Hawaii State House of Representatives? *No one wants the ghost of Christmas past lurking about with unwelcome advice*, he thought.

Bill did still cling to those stimulating days studying premodern Korean history. He remembered a well-known book on how the Dutch had shipwrecked on Cheju Island in the 17th century, and saw the cement monument to them along the coast. His middle school English co-teachers had teased him about how they were his ancestors, but he just laughed it off. Something to talk about after a few hours of Korean rice liquor, soju, and raw fish in a local drinking hole.

But now, maybe it would be worth trying to dig into this Dutch thing. But Mongol? Doesn't make sense, he reasoned.

One night, bored and unable to sleep, he Googled Korean English language newspapers, and found the on-line *Cheju Monthly*, which carried a summary of local stories, with a web site that could translate them into English. It was a vastly different Island from when he lived there during his Peace Corps days, not the least of which was the fact that the population had virtually doubled since then.

Most of the recent controversies swirled around outside investors pushing high rise casinos. One caught his eye. It was a dispute over a proposal to build a 35-story luxury condo and casino right behind one of the most ancient buildings on Cheju: The Kwandokjong – a 15th century pavilion right in the center of Cheju City. He remembered it fondly. An all-wooden open-air pavilion with traditional curved tile roof shingles, and colorful wooden eaves, where on rare occasions in the 70s official ceremonies sponsored by the Cheju government were held.

"What an obscenity to build a casino there," he'd emailed Ted. It was the oldest structure on the Island, and declared a National Treasure. Apparently, there was a legal ambiguity as to the actual owner of that property. He mentioned this to Eiko, who usually grounded him in reality.

"You are not going to let this go, are you?" she asked. "Are you having another short nostalgic memory or is this your second midlife crisis?" she chided.

"Well, yeah, maybe. But it's fun. Of course its ancient history, and ego, and remembering when I was young, and rekindling those Peace Corps friendships."

"By the way, for your birthday coming up, several weeks ago I did a deep dive search into some of the ancestors identified for you. I went to the Amsterdam Historical Society which includes a major collection of Dutch East Indian and other navigators in the past. I may as well tell you, since you may get stuff in the mail, but it's possible that your great grandfather, who you were kind of named after, well his brother's name wasn't Hamilton, it was *Hamelldon!!* Ring a bell? Hendrick Hamel on Cheju? How about that, Mr. Historian? I thought you would get a kick out of it. Hoping the documents will arrive in time for your birthday, honey bun. But boy, were those folks suspicious and bureaucratic when I was there. This form, that form. They said they must report on all such information requests and that it would be on some web site."

"But that's not all, sweetie. Did you know that there is a statue here in Amsterdam of a Dutch guy who got stranded in Cheju 16 years before Hamel? He never left Korea, and even became a Choson citizen. Must have had a bunch of offspring there. Korean name was Pak won. His real name was Jan Janse de Weltevree. The statue is in this tiny Dutch village of De Rijp. So, turns out, there is this odd connection between Holland and Cheju and Korea. And Hamel mentions in his journal that they actually met. You wonder if Hamel or any of his returning crew brought any Koreans back with them, as in wives or kids."

"You're kidding? Really?" He gave her a big kiss and hug. She pushed him away and reminded him about recaulking the shower, a promised handyman chore he'd been putting off. "I've got to get going to meet my friend Carol for lunch. I'll pick up some takeout food for dinner. See you later," she said as she went out the door.

Bill pondered this new revelation and wondered if he needed to recalibrate his understanding of his family ancestry and his heritage. Could it be that….no, that would be too fantastic to actually be related, and to even have long lost ties to Cheju that he never imagined.

It was after six pm when Bill returned to their apartment. Odd that the lights weren't on. He opened the door and flicked on the light. The apartment was a mess. Furniture overturned. Contents of drawers all over the floor. Someone had ransacked every room, and no sign of Eiko. The filing cabinet in his home office was turned over and virtually all the papers and files were dumped in a pile. He peeked into the bathroom. Scrawled on the mirror with one of Eiko's lipsticks was the following message:

If you want to see your wife again, come to the canal in front of the Ann Frank House at midnight. Come alone.

**

Chapter 3. I'm Goin Where The Sun Is Shining...

K.C. Sohn looked over his notes before heading out for an exclusive interview with the acknowledged head of the protest in Cheju City, Ko Tae-jung.

It wasn't his usual beat for the Oakland Asia Times Seoul Office. He had been in Korea for six months, sent primarily to cover the stories of North Korean defectors. He'd grown up in a typical California Koreatown and spoke Korean pretty well since his father's restaurant operated almost exclusively in their language, with a clientele that was nearly all native speakers.

K.C. had spent his junior year at the University of Washington in Seoul, where he managed to work as a volunteer reporter for a college on-line newspaper. He was hooked, and later enrolled in the exclusive Portland College of International Languages, where he not only honed his Korean language skills, but added a robust understanding of Japanese and Cantonese dialect Chinese.

For K.C., Korea was Seoul, Seoul was Korea. Being sent down to Cheju was, in his view, like being in exile.

"K.C., I need you to find out what is going on down there," his editor, Doo-sung Kang, told him. "We've got these hugely powerful Chaebol conglomerates like the Sogwip'o Corporation partnering with the Chinese Xian Development Group pouring foreign money into the Island, massive demonstrations, and the apparent assassination of the Vice Governor."

"Are you sure its worth the time? Can't we just wait and see how it all plays out?" pleaded Sohn.

"No can do. Oakland wants to make a splash. They want to get on the map for covering the East. You spent two years in Osaka and some of your stories were on the Korean/Cheju community there. You arguably have connections. You might score interviews because you know their relatives. Just give it a try. You'll be back here in the center of Korea's political vortex soon enough."

"Yeah, but the presidential election is coming up and I have an inside contact in one of the campaigns," Sohn pleaded.

"So, get your ass down there and get the story, then you can come back."

Sohn was lucky enough to book a room in the Harubang Hotel, overlooking the main public street and square in front of Cheju's oldest Choson Dynasty building, the Kwan-dok-jong Hall, built in 1443 as a military training facility. Off to the side you could see a fairly recent reconstruction of a Choson Dynasty governmental complex, the Cheju Mok-Gwan-a, with several buildings, opportunities dress up in traditional Korean clothes for a picture, and providing opportunities providing for visitors to observe re-creations of traditional weddings.

He was looking down on the scene as 5,000 angry protestors held a noisy rally to protest the plan to build a massive casino immediately behind the pavilion. There were speeches. Homemade signs reading Stop the TCH in Korean, referring to the shorthand for the T'amna Casino & Hotel. As the demonstration reached a fever pitch, radicals climbed the fence in front of a post office, cut their fingers, and wrote in blood: *Free T'amna!*, *Free T'amna!*- referring to an ancient name of the Island.

He took a picture of the pavilion from his hotel the day after the demonstration.

His editor was not without clout, so through convoluted channels, a friend of a Cheju college professor, he had been able to set up an interview with one of the leaders of the demonstration.

His supposed contact for the interview was to pick him up at 9 pm. He waited in the car port, somewhat uneasy about the late hour. A taxi rolled up. Someone in the back seat said "Get in."

It was a short ride past the East Gate Market up the wooded hill overlooking the city known as Sarabong Park. The Taxi turned off a small road and wound its way to an isolated farmhouse with a thatched roof. Sohn was escorted into the front door. The living room area was clean but modest, and he was told to sit down on a kitchen chair and wait. After five minutes a young woman in her late 20s came out of the back room and sat opposite.

"You are K.C. Sohn. Do you have ID?" He showed her his credentials.

"OK Sohn. My name is Pu Kyung-ok, she said in English. Ko Tae-jung is busy. I'm sitting in for him. I'm on the Stop TCH Steering Committee. Our efforts are on behalf of a coalition of groups across the island. Mine is the Shin-Song Alumni Alliance. Others are the Pyoson Diving Women's Cooperative, the Udo Resistance Club, and several other organizations. Are you getting this?

Sohn was busy scribbling on his reporter's tablet and turning on his cell. He looked up. "I was under the impression that I'd be interviewing Ko. Is there are reason he isn't here? Was he injured? Was he arrested?"

"Don't get ahead of yourself. There is nothing Ko knows that I don't know." She said 'Leave Us' in Korean to an associate who was observing. He left the room.

"Look, I don't appreciate being manipulated, but I'm going to conduct this interview as if you were Ko, and I'm going to begin by asking about who you are and why you are involved."

"Fair enough," answered Pu. "But before you start, I do have a request, and it's about how you write about us. Most of the official government and tourist names for the island spell it: **Je**ju. This is so wrong. In English you lose the ch sound in the first letter. We are not like **ju**ice, we are more like **Ch**eese. Got it? Before the crazy Seoul linguists mutilated how Korean was written in English letters, we were Cheju, with the Ch sound. So we want you to agree to refer to the Island as either Cheju or its ancient name T'amna. Are you OK with that?"

"Your English is excellent."

"Syracuse University, class of 2016, a degree in East Music & Art Studies."

"Ok, Ms. Pu, if I may call you that. What is this Shin-Song Alumni group? Are you radicals, communists, socialists, environmentalists, nationalists, or what?"

"Shin-Song is one of the most prominent private girls' Catholic schools in Cheju City. It was always run essentially by Irish Columban Missionary Priests. They hired the best teachers, especially English teachers. They promoted free thought. They even promoted music. They quietly supported opposition candidates, including former Korea President Kim Dae-jung when he first ran against the tyrant Park Chun-hee. The school has moved up the mountain to so-called New Cheju, the missionaries have left, and the reference to Alumni is in honor of our parents. All our members are children of the previous generation's grads."

"And Syracuse? Kind of far away."

"My aunties were Cheju diving women. They had their own work songs I learned as a kid. I had a good singing voice. A Priest at my high school had a connection with Syracuse. His brother went there and played the trombone. Got me into their music and arts school. But I never use that training. It was the Maxwell School of Pollical Science that really inspired me. And the Native American tribes in upstate New York. I even had your radical future U.S. Senator Jackie Saunders in one of my classes. OK, enough stalling, let's get to what you want to know about Cheju."

She's kind of cute in a feisty sort of way, he thought. "OK. Tell me the short version about the reasons for your protests."

I like his eyebrows' she thought. *'No, don't get distracted,'* she told herself.

"First, you've got to understand our history, and I don't mean what happened this week or last year. Cheju has also seen itself with this kind of belonging - kind of an independent island. For centuries China, Japan, and the rulers on the Korean mainland tried to pretend that we belonged to them. Time and time again we resisted. Official historical records written in Chinese mention major rebellions in 932, 1105, 1153, 1269, 1273, 1316, 1368....well, here, I made a list of all those. Right up to the infamous genocide of the 4-3 (April Third) Rebellion in 1948. The point is that T'amna, and later Cheju Province, always resisted attempts to dominate."

"OK, I'm impressed by your history, but I'm not here to talk about ancient history, I'm here to talk about yesterday," said Sohn with genuine irritation in his voice.

"I know, you hot shots from Seoul don't want to hear it. You want to sweep in, get some tasty Cheju food, get a good quote or two, and write a story that has a snappy headline. You don't give a shit, pardon my Upstate NY language, about us. You probably can't wait to get back to your lavish digs in Seoul."

"That's unfair. But I'm not going to waste my time listening to your rant about why Cheju is pure and Seoul is corrupt. Let's get to the point. What are the main issues?"

"OK, are you taking notes? Recording? The Kwandokjong Pavilion (the Chinese characters mean literally Hall of Virtue) was built during Choson's King Sejong reign, in the mid 15th century, as a military training facility. Don't tell me you don't know who he was? Inventor of the Korean phonetic alphabet? Never mind. Well, it was apparently built when Cheju City was just a small outpost. At most at another location there was a small fortress or castle along the coast. The Pavilion was built by People's Commander Shin Sook-chung on land owned by one of the early administrators, kind of a governor, called a *Moksa*. It's possible he also owned lots of land around it as well. You know, from the times of the Silla Dynasty – 5th, 6th, 7th century - on the mainland the losers in political fights were sent to Cheju, and all kinds of lands were essentially stolen from the local residents. The official records were often not kept, or lost, or intentionally destroyed."

"For the record, I AM recording this on my cell. Are you saying that part of the fight over the casino involves a dispute over who actually owns the land nearby and has the right to build?

"Possibly. I'd LIKE to say **definitely**. We suspect it could be true. But so far, we can't prove it. It's not just a legal case. At this point, we've got to push back and delay, delay, delay. It's a political fight. It's a cultural fight. It's Island pride. It's respecting the people of Cheju, who cherish that site, that pavilion."

"One thing I've noticed," said Sohn. "The history of land use I've been told has a strong anti-Japanese flavor. Is some of this lingering resentment about the colonization and later the war?"

"I can't deny we have some resentments. But you should keep in mind that both the Korean and Japanese governments had very low opinions of Cheju. In 2007 a couple of scholars wrote an interesting paper about our autonomy, and subjugation by everyone. They regarded us as militant, barbaric, and distant. Disrespect, bullying, exploitation…its an old story. But I have to confess, maybe militant is not so far off."

Pu paused and looked into K.C. Sohn's eyes, hoping to see a flicker of genuine interest and empathy. But she could not read his expression. Was he really Korean or more American? He was probably in his mid-thirties. Young enough to be independent, yet old enough to have bought into the establishment. *Ambitious*, she thought. *But still fairly professional*.

"So, you are Korean American?" she asked.

"Yes. I grew up in a Korean family in California, travelled to Korea and Japan. Learned the language pretty well. Drifted into journalism. Honestly, I don't know much about this island today or the history you so passionately love…"

"Don't patronize me, Sohn. You think what we are doing is driven by emotion? Yes, we feel. We hurt. But our actions are based on analysis, on conviction, on a history of abuse and attempts to dominate us. We are not quaint pie in the sky dreamers. We are grounded in the reality of the exploitations we can document. We are grounded in the leverage, the power, the roots of Cheju traditions of independence and pride. So, please don't reduce us to emotional children. "

K.C. paused and looked up at her. She was not what he first expected. She and whoever she represented were serious. Consequential. They meant to change things, and they meant to stop the damn casino. He wondered how far they would go to do it.

"Can we talk about the Vice Governor? Lee Yong-Ho was apparently beaten and his body found at Dragon Head Rock along the shoreline?"

"No, we cannot. We had nothing to do with that. We are not criminals. But to be honest he was corrupt and abused his power, had at least three mistresses, and bent the law to benefit his cronies. We nicknamed him the *T'amna Turd*, because you could smell his filthy dealings from far away."

"Why won't Ko Tae-jung see me? No disrespect, but why send you?"

Pu laughed quietly to herself and rolled her eyes. "You've got a lot to learn about Cheju. You've not done your homework, Mr. K.C. Sohn. On this island, women are not afterthoughts just taking care of the kids. We are often the main breadwinners, especially in families with diving women. Diving women are strong. We learn to hold our breath for five minutes in warm and cold water as we dive without tanks to harvest abalone and other sea creatures. We are the heart of the economy for coastal villages. We are organized into small cooperative groups. We finance each other. We support each other and are often the defacto leadership in a village. When Japan held Korea as a colony, back in 1931 over 17,000 diving women protested a Japanese controlled diving association. It was Korea's largest protest movement ever led by women."

"I thought farming was dominant."

"Not necessarily in every section of the Island. You've got the green rice and bright yellow rapeseed flowers alternating all over the mountain in the spring. Beautiful. But fishing has always been a respected and needed source of food and income here. Not just for Cheju, but for other nations who send their fleets in our direction. For centuries. And sometimes those foreign so-called fishing vessels came armed, so it was sometimes hard to distinguish them from out-and-out pirates. It's complicated."

"You were quick to change the subject away from the Vice Governor. Do you know who did it?"

"Do you think I am stupid? If I knew, would I tell a blabbermouth and his cell phone? Whoever did it, would be angry if we told what we knew, that is, if we knew anything."

"Let me ask another way. Was the Vice Gov mixed up in this casino business?"

"I think this interview is over. Mr. Ko has no need to speak with you. We will be reading your paper to see if you got the story right. We will be watching. Goodbye, Mr. Sohn." She abruptly stood and left the room.

Sohn sat there alone for ten minutes contemplating the discussion. Wondering what was not said. Wondering if he was the one being interviewed to see what he knew. Eventually, he went out the front door in the dark and discovered he had to find his way back to the main road and walk down the hill back into the city.

***

Chapter 4. Book Em.

Bill's nervous discussion with the Amsterdam police gave him some assurance that they would do all they could to ensure his wife's recovery without harm. "Video monitoring and 24/7 patrols would be covering the site," said Inspector Bakker. He emphasized that these situations were often fraught with danger as they didn't know the mental state or the willingness to commit violence by kidnappers.

Bakker's cell phone rang.

"Bakker, this is Van Dijk."

"Got it, Chief."

"Any evidence or hints that this is about money? Amsterdam has so many abductions over getting even financially or paying alimony."

"Nothing like that so far."

"Look Bakker, if this is another dead end that we can't solve in a day or two, I'm taking you off the case. We can't waste our time and resources without a solid lead. Don't discourage the husband, but don't promise anything either."

"Got it Chief."

Hamilton arrived fifteen minutes early opposite the Ann Frank House. In the canal there was a houseboat, typical of so many canal vehicles. But it appeared that no one was in it. Otherwise… nothing. No hint of any contacts.

Suddenly, a motor scooter came racing down the road and tossed a plastic bag at Hamilton. In a flash, it was gone. Inside, a note:

Hamilton, we told you to come alone, not with half the police force. If you want to get your wife back in good health, don't cross with us again. Go to the front of the train station. To the right of the door is a trash can. Inside is a package for you. Don't screw up.

Police Inspector Bakker read the note. He immediately directed units to descend on the train station to see if they could catch the kidnappers. Hamilton was driven there in a police car. He leapt out of the car and ran to the trash can. In it was a manilla envelop. He ripped it open. Inside was a cell phone with a short YouTube video link. He clicked on the link.

"*Hello Willie,*" said his wife, with a shaky voice. She was holding up a current newspaper with the day's date to prove she was still alive. *"I'm Ok. I'm in a hotel but I don't know where."*

The video went silent but panned around the hotel room which appeared to be a moderate but modern and clean studio, typical of thousands throughout Amsterdam. It was taken at night so there was no way of knowing where it was, or what direction it faced.

Eiko was then seen to be reading from a script she

had in front of her. *"Willie, they want you to go to the Amsterdam Naval Archives Museum and find a diary written by a cousin of Hendrick Hamel in the 17th century. They want you to find the diary then wait for instructions when you get it. They will contact you on this phone. The people holding me will know if you do this. Please do it soon. I want to be released unharmed, but...."* The video went dead.

"OK Mr. Hamilton," said Inspector Bakker, "is there anything about this video that you noticed, about your wife, how she was dressed, her voice, anything."

"One thing. She never, never calls me Willie. I am always Bill. William was what her mom used to call me, and her mom, well, we really didn't get along at first. I wasn't good enough for her daughter, at first. Maybe Eiko was maybe trying to tell me that things were not good for her. So, William might make sense, but not Willie."

"Chief, this is Bakker. These guys sound like fruitcakes. Go to a museum and look something up? I'm not sure this is for real."

"OK Bakker. Keep me informed, but again, don't waste too much time on this. We still have that bank robbery to solve."

Bill Hamilton sat on his bed in the Hotel New Amsterdam. He played the video from the untraceable burner phone over and over. Eiko looked frazzled and frightened. But she was a strong woman. She was trying to tell him something by calling him Willie. Detective Bakker didn't seem to be deeply interested or concerned.

Why are they sending me to a museum? Can it be that related, possibly, to learning more about my heritage?

This seems strange. Is someone using me to get documents they can't get themselves? Why would you kidnap someone for documents? Am I just a pawn in some larger scheme we don't know about? Is this about insurance?

He tried to sleep but tossed and turned all night. Tomorrow he would go to that museum. Inspector Bakker agreed to pick him up and they would go together. Nothing made sense.

**

It took Hamilton and Bakker more than an hour waiting for the museum clerk to track down the diary. It was in a protected and private section that the public could not access. It took a bit of prodding and a special phone call to the Chief Museum Curator to convince him that accessing this extremely rare book written in archaic Dutch would be permitted. Finally, it was agreed that they would be able to "see" the book in a special sterile room, wearing special gloves, under the direct supervision of an archivist.

"It won't do you any good to look at it since you won't be able to read it," said the archivist in Dutch. "As we explained, the diary is written in old Dutch language. It would take hours to translate a few pages, assuming our expert is available." Hamilton could speak some local modern dialect but some of the vocabulary came too fast for him.

"Look, we can't get caught up in red tape," said Bakker in his best intimidating official voice in English. "We need to borrow this book, for a short time, and we need to get ahold of you translator, who we need to bring with us. This is about a major crime that is possibly life threatening. Do you understand?"

"Fill out this form. I'll run it up to the Chief Museum Curator for approval. Ten minutes. But you better take good care of it. It is one of our gems in the older collection. You damage it, the insurance company is going to throw you into the canal at midnight."

He's right about that insurance thing, thought Bill.

Bakker and Hamilton waited patiently on a very hard wooden bench. The phone from the kidnappers rang. A link led them to a voice recording in English.

Take the book to the Starbucks Café on the second floor of the Tourist Information Center next to the McDonald's on Netherlands Avenue. Ask for Sven. Give the book to him, order your coffee and wait. Don't try anything funny. We will be watching. We still have your wife.

Thirty minutes later, the archivist came back with the book inserted into a sealed, plastic envelope.

"My supervisor says a rude police person pressured the Curator to allow you to borrow this rare and expensive book for 24 hours. Our Curator is a good friend of the Mayor. If this book is not in my hands by noon tomorrow, you will regret it."

Hamilton and Bakker left immediately.

***

Chapter 5. Rebels With A Cause

After filing his initial story with Seoul Oakland Asian Times, K.C. Sohn spent his morning strolling through the East Gate Market building in Cheju City. It was an old musty concrete structure built during the Japanese occupation. You could buy just about anything, including clothes, bedding, and kitchenware, from the tiny stalls and niches, and you could still bargain for the price. It was part of the joy of a small business in a small town.

He collected hats on his many travels, so he spotted a Cheju cap dyed with persimmon extract. He enjoyed chatting with the middle-aged Cheju lady selling them. He asked about the persimmon dye, and she told him it was a traditional way of waterproofing clothes. She wanted the Korean won equivalent of $25. He said it was worth only $10. She went into a loud rant about how tourists like him didn't respect Cheju people, always exploiting them. It was hard to understand her as she was obviously speaking with a heavy Cheju dialect. But they went back and forth, and others in nearby booths drifted over to enjoy the competition. Finally, he said he could not pay more than $15 and she said SOLD. Her fellow small business friends now almost surrounding him, gave him a round of applause.

"You tourist first time Cheju?" she said in Korean.

"Not really. A reporter."

The owner of the shop perked up. She went to a bookshelf and brought out a thin volume that was titled: Cheju Traditional Culture and History, by a Professor Chin.

"Hey mainland news boy, you need this book, eh. This book teach you about Cheju. You better understand us, yeah? I give you this book by my uncle Chin, eh, who used to run a museum, eh. You read and understand. You read and respect, eh You know about that demonstration? All about land and money. Uncle Chin had his own little museum, did all this research and kept artifacts and records and wrote books. You know what those sonabitches did? They drove him out and built their own fancy concrete museum on his property. They kicked him out. Stole his land."

"What happened to him?" Sohn was straining to keep up and understand the local Cheju dialect.

"He moved out of the city near the coastal village of Hamdok, in a traditional thatched roof house. But his heart was broke. He lost hope. Died a sad man. Sonsabitches."

"How much for the book?" They haggled over a price.

"Fo you, fo you git to know Cheju, 5,000 won."

"OK. Here. Thanks for this. I'll read it. I promise."

**

Sohn wandered past the main rotary in town and turned down a small alley to one of Cheju's oldest shopping streets, a narrow shopping sidewalk originally built barely wide enough for the old three wheeled weekly honeydipper trucks to navigate in sucking up individual shop and housing sewage, common in the last century.

The shops were small, and you could see that some of them still had a raised back room with sliding shoji doors where the owners apparently slept. While the heyday of tea rooms was long gone, there were still a few upscale pastry and coffee shops on second floors above as part of the desperate attempt to keep this traditional street, known as Seven Star Street (C'hil Song Tong) financially viable. Cheju scholars and historians traced this street back two centuries. He glanced up and noticed that a renovated building had once been a movie theater in an earlier age, back when the promotions were hand painted artistic renderings of the film and its stars.

"That's the guy. That's him," said Pu looking down from the 2nd story pastry shop overlooking the strolling tourists below.

"The one you met the other night?" asked Ko. "Can he be trusted?"

"Well, he's basically a tool of the Seoul news establishment. Remains to be seen if he will listen. You look weak today, Ko. Did you have chemo today?"

"Never mind me. Focus on the plan. I know you were uneasy with abducting the woman, even though we made it clear she would be treated well. She is doing well. Don't leave any loose ends. This guy is one piece of the puzzle to achieve our ultimate goal. To stop that damn casino. Have you heard anything from Europe?"

"Nothing. They promised to call after the Times runs an article on our protests."

***

Oakland Asia Times – Seoul Edition
K.C. Sohn reporting from Cheju Island, Korea

CHEJU REBELS AGAIN
A Troubled Island with a Violent Past Erupts in Protests Over A New Casino

Cheju Island, some 90 miles off the Korean southern coast, lived up to its historical reputation as a feisty, hard-to-govern and hard-to-control outpost of the Korean presence in the Korea Strait. Known in its tourism promotions as having an abundance of Wind, Women, and Rocks, the reality is that the people of Cheju, from the fifth century on, have fiercely resisted attempts to control or govern it, going back to the fifth century Silla, Koryo, and on to Choson, the Japanese occupation, and modern Korea. Literally hundreds of years.

Originally known as the independent Kingdom of T'amna, neither the mainland Korean governments nor the occupying Mongols in the 1200s and 1300s, could fully control its population of farmers, diving women and fishermen. Cheju was a convenient place to exile the losers of political clashes. It was taken over by Mongols who used the Island as a breeding ground for their horses until 1356.

Major protests and violent resistance battles are noted in 1105, 1153, 1269, 1271, 1273, 1316, 1356, 1368, 1395, and on and on including the near genocide in 1948 when an estimated 30,000 lives were lost in clashes between the conservative Syngman Rhee troops and suspected communists.

Residents erupted once again yesterday, as over 5,000 of Cheju[s 600,000 residents gathered in the heart of Cheju City to protest the plan to build a huge high-rise casino and luxury hotel overlooking a cherished ancient Choson era pavilion.

This reporter interviewed one of the leaders protesting the casino plan, a young woman named Pu Kyung-ok. Pu had attended an American university in New York, and insisted we speak in English. When asked what the issues were, Pu, who is descended from a clan of traditional diving women, spoke passionately about the economic exploitation of Cheju, its people, and its land by Korean mainland conglomerates in league with foreign investors, most of whom were from China.

When asked about the recent apparent assassination of Cheju's Vice Governor. Pu and she said her protestors vehemently deny having a hand in his brutal beating and death. She claims there is no connection between that crime and her protests.

At the heart of the development controversy is the belief by the Stop TCH Steering Committee, TCH stands for T'amna Casino Hotel that the developers may not have clear title to the large plot of land planned for the development, scheduled to break ground in six months. When challenged to produce any credible proof of this assertion, Pu had none to share.

This reporter also interviewed a representative of the Sogwip'o Development Group, known as SDG, one of the main partners in the project. Mr. Hong Dae-shik is a very soft-spoken businessman.

"Mr. Sohn, I am a Cheju boy who just wants to bring prosperity to my home. Of course, change, especially economic change, that is manifested by a new and unfamiliar altering in the landscape such as a new hotel, is often initially resisted. People are nostalgic about the Island of their youth. There were massive protests when we started to create the magnificent Chungmun Prosperity District on the south shore. But now, so many of the resisters have jobs in those hotels and condos. Change is hard, especially for an island that has its own subculture, even its own distinct language or dialect."

"Why did you decide to build this casino and hotel so close to the iconic Kwan-dok-jong Pavilion, which is cherished by local residents?"

"Cheju City is the place for such a landmark architectural and economic statement. Cheju City needs to emerge from the dusty faded memories of ancient Korea and join its brother cities on the mainland in a dynamic, modern Korea that is the new hub of East Asia."

Hong came prepared with expensive multicolored renderings of the future building, which included estimates of how much money, jobs and general prosperity would be infused into Cheju. Each day I sit down and recalculate the legitimate costs, he said with pride. He also, with obvious false modesty, provided detailed financial projections on the actual cost of the project on expected profits for the first five years.

Whether the TCH can muscle its grand scheme without setbacks in the land issue remains to be seen.

***

Chapter 6. Sven Who?

"Dad, you've got to be kidding. Mom was actually kidnapped? How? Why? Is she ok?" Masato Hamilton was speaking from a WhosAPP video feed. He was obviously distressed when he got the call from his father in Amsterdam.

"Son, all we know is that somehow it *may* be connected to her looking for our family roots and ancestors who had a Dutch name that was at some point converted to a more English spelling. Or it may be connected to my current job or employer. As I said, somebody ransacked our condo, and has been directing us to find an obscure book written by a guy who was sailing around Korea and Cheju centuries ago."

"What the heck are the police doing?"

"They are working on it, holding my hand, but I suspect there are so many crimes in this city they are not going to put a lot of resources into finding your mom. I may have to take the initiative, but I think you can help."

"How? I'm stuck here in Hawaii! We are in the middle of a legislative session. Do you want me to fly out to Amsterdam?"

"Not yet. Remember I told you there was once a sister state agreement between Cheju and Hawaii? Well, using that as justification, I think we need to know more about the older history of Cheju, especially how their legal system works with land use, and who owns it, and how choice pieces of real estate were passed from owner to owner down the generations. I suspect, only a gut feeling at this point, that somebody thinks I may have a distant claim to something in Cheju. It's just a hunch, but if you can get someone at the University of Hawaii, maybe the law school, to dig into how that might work, who knows, maybe its connected."

"So, what is your next step over there?"

"Somebody is sending us on a wild goose chase relating to an old diary, and the kidnappers, whoever the hell they are, are using Mom as leverage to get me to find something they want. But to tell you the truth, neither I nor the police know if this has something to do with the insurance business I'm in, or something else. Maybe that book is insured and valuable and they want to sell it on the black market to an obscure collector."

"Of course, I'll get right on it. Can you call me again at the end of your day to tell me anything new?"

"Of course. This is so unbelievable. My mind is still in a bit of a fog trying to process it all. On the video, Mom even called me Willie."

"OK, Dad. Love you."

"Love you too."

**

Hamilton had gone outside the café to the street to take his son's call. He didn't really want Inspector Bakker listening in, and wanted to be completely candid with his son about whether he completely trusted the commitment of the police.

"Family call, Hamilton?"

"Yeah, my son in Hawaii. Did I mention he is a state legislator? He's obviously extremely worried about his mother. Frankly, he had a lot of questions about what you guys are doing to get her back safe and sound."

After another coffee refill, a middle aged, very well-dressed businessman approached.

"Are you Mr. Hamilton?"

"Yeah, who are you?" asked Bakker.

"My name is Sven. I am instructed to receive a book from Mr. Hamilton, that I will take temporarily to a secure room in the back of this establishment to inspect for authenticity and photocopy key pages. I will return it to you within 30 minutes."

"You got ID?" barked Bakker, obviously annoyed and wanting to communicate who was in charge.

"I am Sven. That is all I am instructed to communicate. Are you going to loan me the book or shall I notify my associates to abort this transaction?" He stared with steely eyes through his large rimless glasses.

Hamilton handed over the book. "30 minutes."

Sven quickly walked to the back of the shop and disappeared through a back door.

"We've got this place under surveillance, Hamilton. No way this Sven or whatever his name is can pull a fast one. We also have operatives placed discretely at street level."

Hamilton glanced out the window to the street. A woman with a backpack and a helmet was seen revving up a motorbike and driving off. No one challenged her.

After 45 minutes, Bakker summoned their waiter. "Can you ask your associate named Sven to get back out here?"

"Sven? We have no Sven. Never heard of him. Are you sure you haven't misheard his name? We do have a cook named Swenson. Do you want to talk with Swenson?"

Bakker bolted from the table and charged for the door in the back while talking on his phone. The door led to a corridor with two other doors. One was a supply closet. The other led to stairs leading down to the street. "Damn it."

Hamilton was visibly distraught. "You mean with all your cops you let this fictitious guy get away with this book, the book that might be necessary to get my wife back? What the fuck is the matter with you, Bakker?"

"Watch your mouth, Hamilton. Just shut up and follow our instructions. We can't afford to have you peppering us with questions and insults. Let us do our job. I'm going to have Officer Visser take you back to your hotel, where you will sit tight and not get in our way, understand?"

These guys have blown it, and they are trying to cover up their screw up, thought Bill.

When he got back to his hotel room, Bill Hamilton knew that the life of his wife Eiko could be in real danger. *If the kidnappers got what they were after, this stupid book, would they still need his wife? What the hell was this all about? And what was she trying to tell him by calling him Willie?*

***

Chapter 7. Bleached

"K.C. we have another small assignment for you while you are down there in the Hawaii of the East," said his Seoul editor, Kang Doo-sung.

"Did you like the article I sent?"

"It was OK, but you know now you've got to find out how the people of Cheju, especially the protestors, are going to respond. But that's not why I called. We got a tip that there is a really interesting land use court case going on down in Sogwip'o."

"OK, Doo-sung. But don't you usually have someone who usually follows the law cover those?" Sohn was actually happy to get out of Cheju City and down to the fantastic beaches on the southern side of the egg-shaped island. He'd heard that Chungmun Beach was not to be missed.

"The court is going to convene tomorrow at 2 pm. A major developer is making a claim that he has the right to develop a sweet land parcel because he has a very old deed that dates back, are you ready for this, the 17th century. It's quite a story, if you can believe the preliminary briefs. Even the Mongols who took over Cheju 200 years before are referenced."

"OK, OK. I'll get a bus. Do I have permission to check into a hotel down there?"

"Whatever you need to do to get the story. Attend the hearing. See if you can get an interview. This might be a dead end, or too convoluted for our readers, but you just never know."

Oh Boy, some nice beach time, he thought. It was a pleasant enough bus ride out of Cheju City, up up towards the impressive dominant Mt. Halla in the center of the Island, past the grassy pastures, and down toward Chungmun, and the aging but recently refurbished Chungmun Hyatt Hotel, located on a bluff above a spectacular beach.

K.C. checked in and quickly changed into his swimsuit and headed down the steep steps to the beach. After a refreshing swim, he wandered to the eastern side of the beach and up to a small cave. Just outside was a small concession stand selling upscale juices and snacks. He bought something to drink, when he heard a familiar voice.

"So, you think we are all a bunch of troublemakers, huh, Sohn?"

He swung around and found the protestor Pu Kyung-ok staring at him. She was wearing a terrycloth robe that only partially covered a bikini. Sohn's eyes took in the pleasant sight.

"Do you think I was unfair?"

 She noticed his athletic upper body.

"It's not that you were unfair. It's that you were kind of superficial. You reported on the press release from the developer, but not the real story, Sohn. It was a start, I suppose."

"Have you been following me?"

"Let's say we may have the same reason to be in Sogwip'o this afternoon. We have friends in Seoul, and we suspected you might be sent to cover the court hearing."

They walked slowly down the slope from the cave, over a steep sand dune, and sat down close to the breaking waves. The beach was full of tourists, and there were surfers just beyond the reef. The smell and misty spray of the salt water filled the air.

"Is this your favorite beach? Do you live near here?" asked Sohn.

I hope this is not going to turn into a pickup attempt, she wondered. *Would I really mind?*

"It's a famous beach. My auntie was a diving woman near here and we used to visit them during summer vacation. She tells a funny story about how some 45 years ago there were a bunch of American teachers, Peace Corps, and they came to this deserted beach, and were sleeping in the sand. It was pitch dark. No hotels anywhere near here. They were sleeping on the beach out in the open at night, and when they were all asleep the local militia patrols came by - the Y*ebigun*, guns and all. This was a time of great paranoia over North Korea. They literally tripped over the sleepers in the dark. There were screams. There was yelling. It's amazing that no one was hurt. The *Yebigun* guys, hardly out of high school, didn't know what to do with the crazy foreigners. That story was told often locally as we laughed and laughed. It was probably enhanced after several pots of makkoli. Have you had makkoli, a great local milky wine?"

"Oh, so you had the Peace Corps program back then? I heard later Korea started its own version of that."

"Yeah, they were here, but pulled out around 1980. Made a big impression on English teaching apparently. My parents' generation benefited a lot if they had a Volunteer in their middle school. Some of them started a Sister State thing with Hawaii. They promoted a fast-developing tourism, which in my view was not a plus for Cheju. All the Seoul money came down and ruined the Island. Look up along that cliff, that ridge. Hotels and condos blocking our view of Mt. Halla. How much of that really benefited the poor on Cheju is debatable."

K.C. was watching her closely. She was deeply tanned, and he wondered if she was a part time diving woman herself. Her English was pretty good. There was a swagger, a feistiness to the way she spoke. He wondered if most Cheju women had the same self-confidence and strong opinions, or if it was mostly her education back in the U.S.

I've got to concentrate on why I'm here, and not who I'm here with, thought K.C.

"So why are you interested in this court hearing?" he probed.

"Why are YOU interested?"

"Well, my editor wants me to cover it. Seems like it might be an interesting trip through Cheju's ancient history and even back when the Mongols were here. My paper sent me links to the issues being covered in the Cheju papers. For over 100 years the Mongols kind of took over the Island and used it, according to two research papers I read, to raise their horses and plot an invasion of Japan. The horses, the small ones, are still here. The invasions famously failed. That was about the years 1200 and something to 1300 and something. But I'm not sure how that is relevant to today."

At least he is making a faint effort to do his homework, she thought.

"Get real. Do you think your newspaper is really interested in the Mongols? Smarten up Sohn. This is all about land use, big profits, and land abuse. Who owns it. Who can knock down a small farmer's home to build another hotel. Who can prove they once owned it. Who stole it. Who …"

"So, this is, you think, related to the protests over the casino project in Cheju City?"

"Duh. What do you think?"

"Seems like a stretch to me. In a modern society, to put this layman's terms, Korea is very modern, the Japanese and western land systems, documents and all, look similar to most developed countries. Very legalistic. Ownership is more clearly documented. Recognized by a court of law."

"Maybe. Maybe not."

Pu then abruptly tossed down her robe and jogged into the near shore waters. He watched her swim with confidence out and out, then body surfed back into the shore. *This is going to be a day to remember,* he hoped.

**

"What did Sohn say?" asked Ko.

"They took the bait", said Pu. "You were right that the Times would be interested in a related land use story. Knowing that the editor was a history buff made it easier for your lawyer friend to tease him with the Mongol connection. They assigned Sohn to cover it."

"Did you say you spoke with him again?"

"Yeah, I paid my nephew to follow him around, and when he got on the bus to Sogwip'o, he never noticed I was on it too!!"

"OK, great. The more PR we get out of this the better."

***

Oakland Asia Times – Seoul Edition
K.C. Sohn reporting from Cheju Island, Korea

Cheju Government Ownership of Lands Challenged

It was an extraordinary court hearing in Sogwip'o City, Cheju Province. At Issue was the right of a developer to build a hotel and casino in a small agricultural community. At contest was the authenticity and legal validity of centuries old documents.

In The Matter of:

The People of Cheju vs. The Sogwip'o Development Group re Dispute over Clear title to Parcel 34-990, Molsupo Township.

The materials already presented by the plaintiff by their lawyer, Ms. Ku Ga-yun, were of note. Specifically, Ku sought to make the case that the politics and decisions of the 13th and 14th centuries were pertinent to the case.

Relying on the historical research of Professor Ahn No-oon, clan ownership of lands were often complicated by marriages. The court was reminded that when the Mongols dominated the Koryo Dynasty in Korea (935-1392), it was common for Korea royalty to take Mongol queens and concubines. Factions approving or opposing this practice divided whatever unified push back might have diluted Mongol demands. Purges and assassinations were common. In areas that were held in a tighter vice grip by any faction. Cheju saw many intermarriages.

One area of emphasis was that the political and literal DNA of later Koryo Dynasty Korea were heavily marinated by Mongol descendants and practices.

The second area of emphasis was that private landowners, both Korean, Mongol, and even foreigners, were frequently appropriating the lands of royalty, peasants and farmers, leaving those not connected with the Royal Family, as powerless indentured servants or slaves to the owners. The land thefts were often at the direct expense of the local government. Large acreage was transferred to both the Korean and Mongol private winners in political confrontations.

This practice of taking land was continued during the 500 years of the Choson Dynasty (1392-1910). When Choson's King Yi Song-kye became the first King of the new dynasty, many disgruntled Koryo losers were executed.

Attorney Ku asserted that it was almost impossible to determine the rightful owners of many parcels. However, because of this historical reality, the court should not assume that such claims were impossible, nor that those asserting ownership today, including the Cheju Provincial Self-Governing Government, should prevail over those who had documented ownership even a century or more ago.

The Cheju government, represented by Attorney Choe Se-kon, argued that ancient ownership claims were most likely the result of illegal theft, especially when Japan colonized Korea in 1910. He emphasized the overwhelming number of lands transferred to the Cheju government following the departure of the Japanese in 1945.

The Plaintiffs did present a verifiable chain of custody argument attempting to show that the parcels in question have shown up in recognized ownership by a private landowner seven different times. Each example cited by Attorney Ku showed that new buildings or developments were erected with virtually no evidence of these being challenged by Cheju government authorities. In other words, if they didn't object, they tacitly agreed.

In the end, this was a hearing without a definitive decision.

The judge in this case, Yoo-Chung-hee, indicated that he would schedule a subsequent hearing at which further documents could be submitted, additional witness testimony could be heard, and oral arguments were to be made. Briefs were to be submitted in advance of the next hearing.

Professor Ahn, who flew down to Cheju to attend the hearing, spoke to reporters outside the courthouse.

"Efforts to reform the land system at the end of the Koryo period failed because the government needed the support of the big private landowners, many of whom were actually government officials themselves. The vast amount of ag land had passed into estates called *nong-jang*, and the small farmers who had owned the land became tenant farmers and even slaves. When you repeat these travesties again and again you can imagine how you can construct a modern sense of historical justice, or injustice. I really don't know how this is all going to turn out. I'll be reading your reports!" He chuckled.

**

Ku was glad she had done a great deal of research, and her friend who worked at the Pusan City Library had been a great help. For all the legal and historical data, she was drawn to a fragment of an old Peace Corps volunteer journal about a trip to Mosulp'o. Somehow it humanized it all.

March 11, 1970

Mosulp'o is only the local nickname of a settlement in the town of T'aejong. It has 3,000 residents and encompasses two villages. The trip was over incredibly stony roads. The volcanic origins of Cheju are evident by the thousands of lava stone walls surrounding nearly every field. The people must spend a great percentage of their time building and repairing them. The day began with a confrontation with the seemingly lackadaisical and inefficient bus company. The bus left a half hour early, and by the time I did reach Mosulp'o via a later bus I just missed the traditional wedding Ceremony. But the day was not wasted, and I was introduced to all the folks, including Mr. Lee's father. He has five brothers and five sisters. Two brothers have made it big in financial and prestigious terms, both living in Japan, one a doctor, the other a former lawyer and now a businessman."

***

Chapter 8. Loose Ends

How the imposter Sven escaped without notice or transferred the book to his motor scooter collaborator remained a mystery and an embarrassment to Inspector Bakker. Hamilton was very upset. The only positive thing was yet another picture sent anonymously on the burner phone showing Eiko Hamilton holding up yet another current paper.

Bakker asked a linguist friend to ask the museum curator what kind of content might be of interest to a modern criminal. He had the following printout transcript of that interview:

Curator: *"I'm not sure. Part of the early diaries of the first westerners in East Asia often reflected friendly relations and significant gifts in exchange for favorable treatment. We have records of one exchange that paid off for both locals and even foreigners in subsequent years when the local tribes or kings or rulers granted a house and a plot of land. Sometimes this was along the shoreline where the Westerner could build a small pier for a boat. But other times, the local ruler found a political enemy and kicked him off and gave his property to the foreigner. It's possible that the book in question recorded that kind of transaction."*

"Well Chief, sighed Bakker, maybe this is the only thing we have to go on to explain the book. But not the kidnapping. Somehow, we can't link it back to Hamilton."

That afternoon, Bakker received an anonymous text: "Find your book in a red bag next to a bench in front of the Van Gogh Museum." It was there, undamaged. *Whatever they wanted, they must have found.*

"Do you think we can push him that far?"

"We need to at least try. Make him do the leg work. But don't do anything that would connect us down here. Our whole plan depends on keeping all of them guessing. We were lucky to discover his wife's attempt and research. Otherwise, we'd never have even found him."

"When can I return to Cheju?"

"Soon, but not yet. Keep the wife happy, if that's possible. In a few days, if we think it wise, we might let her call him directly."

"How are you feeling?"

"Cancer is not easy. I've got to rely on others. Lots of medications. But please do NOT let our people know my situation."

"Ok, if you insist. If you are really bad, the heck with the plan, go to the Hallim Emergency Room."

**

The phone rang. "Dad, I thought of something."

"Oh, Masato. What?"

"I remember you mentioned that mom called you Willie. I think I know what she was trying to say."

"What?"

"Remember when we visited Washington DC and we stayed at the Wilford Regency? You know I was just a tiny kid. Remember what I called the hotel?"

"Holy shit. You called it Da Willie. You couldn't say Wilford. You called it Da Willie."

"I looked it up Dad. Amsterdam actually has a Wilford Regency Hotel. Here, I'm emailing you the address. Seems to be not that far from those famous museums, like the van Gogh. But wait. I'm not sure it's such a good idea to tell anyone, I mean even the police."

"Why not?"

"I'm not confident it would not somehow leak. We don't want to create a shootem up confrontation, you know? That's the last thing we need. We need to protect Mom from a violent overreaction. So maybe you might try to check out this hotel, you know, discreetly. Get yourself a hoodie or sunglasses and a hat and a leather jacket. Clothes no one would ever associate with a boring uptight insurance guy."

"Am I boring and uptight?"

"Let's not go there, OK? There are some other online sources I think might fill in some of the blanks, especially along the lines of why anyone went after you. There's got to be a connection to the book and the book connects to Cheju. Maybe this links back to your days in the Peace Corps. Did you ever think about that?"

"Yeah, yeah. I've thought of it, but it seems so farfetched. I sent you the Decendents.com info right? But Mongol? C'mon now."

"Let's not rush to judgement one way or the other. Just poke around and play dumb till I get back to you, OK? If you are near that hotel and you see a bunch of Koreans wandering around, maybe my hunch about Da Willie is a real thing."

"Ok, ok. Thanks for keeping on top of this. I'm feeling all alone and helpless. Your call has given me a glimmer of hope."

"Remember, not a word to your Dutch Cop handler."

"Got it. Love you."

"Love you too."

***

Chapter 9. One Year Ago...

Lee Young-Ho was the Vice Governor of Cheju. His rise to this position was facilitated by a group of 12 influential men who formed a clique, an exclusive club, with a special affinity. In Lee's case, they were all graduates of a prominent high school in Cheju City. Later in life, this group of close alumni became landowners, bankers, accountants, developers, promoters of all sorts of political, financial, and economic benefits. They called themselves the Sarabong Gang, because they once frequently met for picnics on that prominent hill overlooking the City.

There was more to the Sarabong Gang than *you help me, I'll help you*. There was a dark side. An enforcement edge that was unforgiving if a member failed to pay back to the common pot the value of what he received. It happened only once. Chang In-jon was once a founding member. The group quietly supported his widow, and tuition for his daughter to attend Ewa University.

From the earliest known records of Korean life there has been a counterpoint to any vertical hierarchy in governance. It began at the highest level of power and privilege, but was also part of traditional village life, where small groups of five or ten families would meet as equals and on a rotating basis provide support and resources to a member. This has been called, in Korean, a *Kye*.

At the top, there was from Silla times (5th-10th centuries) the *Hwabaek* tradition, where the heads of the major clans would meet as equals to reach consensus. Scholars have found the *kye* throughout history and in modern times. A traditional kye distributed its profits or services all at once to members for goals decided by the group. While the geographical connections in a village were driven by common and dependent collective life, in later centuries and urban life a *kye* might well exist in many forms. In Cheju, there were common village level *kye* for diving women. Fishing coalitions, farmers, and especially in the 21st century, political *kye*.

The Sarabong Gang, in the *kye* tradition, had invested tens of millions of Korean won in Lee's political future, and all its influential members expected he would deliver for them. On the collective agenda was the development of the casino business on Cheju, which had been infiltrated by some criminal elements. Lee's job, in the minds of his fellow *kye* members, was to deliver approvals for three major casinos: one on the small island of Udo off the eastern side of Cheju, one on the southern coast, and one in the middle of Cheju City.

A dinner meeting was held in the Cheju Hyatt. There was much happy talk, and the expensive Japanese Soju was consumed in large quantities. Coats and neckties came off. Faces were flushed red. Tables were cluttered with plates of Cheju pork kalbi, kimchee, and seaweed soup bowls. Then the chair of the year clinked his glass, signaling it was time to get down to business.

"Lee, you have let us down," began Hyun P'il-song. "We gave you a hefty advance for Udo, but you let those bastard eco-rebels block it. We paved the way for the Mosilp'o casino, but that seems to have hit a legal complication and delay. Now, we need to see some success for our most important investment in Cheju City. What do you have to say?"

"Listen, I am really sorry that our best efforts…"

"You mean YOUR best efforts."

"My best efforts to repay you all with success haven't panned out yet. But you've got to realize we never, never thought that liberal Moon would become president, or that his distant cousin on Cheju would become an advisor and gain more influence here. We thought he was content to raise tangerines!"

The joke fell flat. All the members of the group were staring at him with frowns.

"We are disappointed, yes. Shit happens, as they say in California. But there is a more serious problem," said Lee. "Perhaps our esteemed senior accountant Pak Jae-min would like to elaborate."

"We gave you a very generous investment amount for these projects. We expected you would use this wisely to, shall we say, encourage support from the Governor, the City administration, and key influencers back in Seoul. That is to be expected. And no, we don't want to know the details. We have agreed not to share such

One Year Ago...

things that would put any of us in danger of knowing too much. *Plausible deniability* the lawyers call it," said Hyun.

"Yes, yes, and I can assure you all that I have done my best to, shall we say, encourage support among those we need," said Lee, obviously nervous.

"Well, as you know, Mr. Kim here is a banker, and he's your banker. And he tells us he discovered that a substantial amount of our investments have gone through your personal account and on to a bank in the Cayman Islands. Do you have an explanation?"

"This is a huge misunderstanding. I'm just trying to protect your, our money. I can assure you that it is just waiting to be used for our projects."

"Lee, I'm sorry. But we have decided that perhaps we need to change our strategy, and invest those millions of Korean won, and converted dollars, in other, more productive directions. In other words, thank you for your efforts but we want, *we demand* our money back. Please transfer all of those funds back to our collective bank trust account."

Lee was visibly shaken. "Listen, if you can just give me a few weeks, maybe a few months to either deliver or pay you back." *God, I hope my gambling debts in Vegas can be wiped out and I can get those won back.*

"You've lost our confidence, Lee Young-ho. But we've been together since high school. You've got till the end of the year to make this right, or...well you can imagine it will not be pleasant for you."

**

Nearly one year to the day from the date of the dinner party, Lee was invited to a small elegant raw fish restaurant just west of the City. It was him and a small group of Gang members and two of their associates whom he had never met. Six hours after a cordial meal, Lee's body was found floating in the near shore jagged coral around Dragon Head Rock.

**

One Month Later….

Cheju City Prosecutor Young Jung-in was sure the murder was the work of those radicals protesting development and was determined to bring them to trial and hopefully punishment. "They are known to be lawless and violent. They disrupt our society. They are against all progress and have no regard for the norms of society. We will get them. YOU will find a way to nail these bastards. I've promised the governor we will bring them to justice," he said to his leadership team. "We will begin by finding a way to bring this communist Ko in for questioning."

***

Chapter 10. Not Far From the Tree...

Alex Masato Hamilton was a newly elected member of Hawaii's State House of Representatives. Elected from a tough urban district bordering the H-1 Freeway on Oahu, he ran on ideas of reform of the process. Hamilton had worked as legislative staff in the Public Access Room, and had successfully obtained funding for a local nonprofit that ran after school clubs promoting international understanding and support for poor villages in the Third World.

His name was Alex, but his Japanese American mother preferred his middle name, Masato, and it stuck. For all his friends in school, and later in his young professional life, it was always Masato, or Masa. He grew up in a family of well-educated progressive politics and service. His father, Bill Hamilton, had been a Peace Corps Volunteer in Korea in the 1970s. His mother, Eiko, was an accomplished researcher with multilingual language skills, who taught him that it may not be enough just to speak English well. If you wanted to understand and contribute, you needed to train your brain to think in different cultural ways.

Masato Hamilton was a member of a group of newly minted reformers that were swept into office following a major scandal that sent five Hawaii Senators to prison. Their collective platform was to frame a Bill of Rights for Citizens who came before the legislature. Respect for all, no bullshit, even distribution of power within, early availability of public testimony, more sunshine, and no backroom decisions to virtually eliminate the public government positions of employees who did not agree to do their bidding – these were some of the so-called *Democracy Culture* civil reforms they embraced. Hamilton knew it would take several sessions before the more powerful legislators accepted any changes to business as usual.

Because he was not yet a committee chair, when the legislature scheduled its yearly five-day recess, Hamilton took the opportunity to book a flight to Cheju. He didn't tell anyone, especially his father. He already had a pretty good idea of who he might try to meet in a short visit. He had, unbeknownst to his parents, found his father's Peace Corps journals in an old cardboard box.

It is rare to have an insight into your young parents, let alone their daily ups and downs in adapting to a very strange and foreign daily life far from Hawaii. Among the papers were initial letters his dad had written to kick start a Hawaii-Cheju Sister State Relationship. Most of such arrangements were merely ego boosting junkets where petty politicians pretended they were big shot foreign ambassadors. Lots of trips. Lots of big elaborate feasts. A tour here or there.

But for Cheju and Hawaii, both took the Sister State arrangement seriously. There were major conferences on planning, economic development, education, and tourism. Some were in Cheju, and some were in Hawaii. More than one governor was involved, on both sides. Over the years, at twenty- or thirty-year anniversaries, new leaders would re-affirm and re-sign vague documents pledging continued good will, friendship and collaboration.

Intertwined in related documents were connections between the University of Hawaii and Cheju National University. There were special connections among Hawaii counties and their planners, along with private planning firms that were paid to assist Cheju in its steep climb out of a poor to a thriving and growing modern economy.

Along the way, according to his father's journals and post Peace Corps correspondence, it was originally very rare for Cheju government workers or teachers to have the money or the permission to fly to Hawaii. But later, looking through the official Hamilton Library archives, a fairly large group of Cheju English teachers did visit Hawaii, a few of whom had actually been co-teachers with his father.

He'd begin there. He'd try to find and connect with and talk with some of these senior retired officials for any clues as to what was going on and why his family had gotten sucked into an actual kidnapping.

**

The aging professor Kim Ki-won was obviously frail. His wheelchair was his main way of getting around the senior center in Cheju. Yet it was obvious his mind was sharp and his English still very polished. He had taught English in a high school, then college, and was for a time the English Language Supervisor for the Island. Multiple trips to the U.S. and even a year in New Zealand had honed his linguistic skills.

"Thank you for seeing me, Professor. I really appreciate your time."

"I remember your father. He was so full of energy. He organized an entire re-write of a TESOL book for college students one summer. An older colleague, now long passed, Professor Kang, was his main booster. Kang made your father a kind of unofficial representative of the other Peace Corps people. That was fine with them because most did not really care about being involved in the educational politics of the day. They were focused on teaching, and were much better in speaking Korean than your father, to be candid. But you did not come all this way to wax nostalgia, eh?"

"What I wanted to talk about was, well, not English or Peace Corps, but some more recent controversies on Cheju. Specifically, the proposal to build a casino here in Cheju City. I wanted to know if you knew anything about who owned or controlled land around it. And especially, how or why, if at all, this could be connected to my family."

Kim, leaned forward, and whispered, "Let's go out on the balcony, where the breeze will cover up our chat." Masato respectfully wheeled Professor Kim through the sliding doors onto the balcony of his private apartment where the Cheju breeze was a barrier to any wannabe eavesdroppers.

"You can't tell anyone your source, agree? Good. Look, you may be probing into what you folks call a can of worms. I grew up on this Island, and my great grandfather was a minor official. This was during the early days of the Japanese occupation of Korea. All officials had to make the hard decision of whether to at least pretend to cooperate with the Japanese officials sent here to strut around the streets and try to tell us what to do. It was a bad time, and we don't really like to talk about it."

"Take your time. Rest assured our conversation is totally confidential. I'm just after basic information."

"This was also a time when many Cheju families were forced to move to the mainland, as their usual occupations or even land were essentially stolen. But I digress."

"No, please. Keep going. This is relevant."

"What was going on was that the emerging new economy in the 30s depended on freeing up city properties to make way for new business. But after the war, a lot of Japanese ownership reverted to the government by default, because no one really knew who originally had the rights to the land. When Japan knew the war was lost, they burned a lot of documents. But, and this is our way of resisting, we made copies of older land ownership deeds. The Japanese were, if anything, pack rats for documentation, mindless documentation if you ask me. You know, to this day, lots of Korean government institutions, schools even, keep lots of records of minor and major importance but they really don't know why. They just do, out of habit, I suppose. There are warehouses in Shin Cheju, the new part of the city up the mountain a bit, filled with documents that no one reads, or wants to read, but just can't throw away. Is this helpful? Boring, huh"

"Candidly, you know my dad was here in the Peace Corps in the 70s, and I know you met him at that time. We kind of suspected that somewhere in our distant past there was a Hamilton relative connected to Cheju. Recently, we've found information and documents to support those possibilities. I'm talking Choson Dynasty and probably before. You see, my father's family came from Europe, and were involved in centuries old shipping and trading. We don't know for sure, but I suspect we may even go back so far as to have distant relatives here. Sailors came and got shipwrecked. They fraternized with locals. Who knows, children distantly related to Europeans may have been brought up here."

"Well, you certainly have a creative imagination. The interesting thing is that Cheju was at the crossroads of lots of Asian and European travelers. I suppose if you did extensive DNA tests of today's population you'd find evidence of Chinese, Japanese, Mongol, and pure Korean families. I'm not sure why this matters. Modern is modern. Old is old. What can you do with that information other than appreciate the mixture that is what we call Asian?"

"This is really helpful. One final question, and then I'll let you go. Is it at all possible that somewhere there would be reliable records about ownership of lands, especially those who are at the center of controversy today?"

"I'll tell you what. I'll give you a name. You can't reveal your source, promise? OK. Well early Europeans were very diligent about keeping records. At Cheju University, there is another old guy like me, who is in charge of a small section of their library. If anyone has a handle on where I think you are going with this, it would be him. Here's his name on this piece of paper. Do not, I repeat, do not tell him where you got this. We used to be friends but after the recent reports and reactions to exposure of the 1948 tragic conflicts in Cheju, well, let's just say we don't talk much anymore."

"Thank you, professor. I really appreciate your time and all the information you've given me. With your permission, I'll try to keep in touch. May I email you in the future? Oh, thank you."

Masato was beginning to get a fuller picture of the history of the Island, and the waves of control and political influence over time. In his next visit, he hoped to fill in more gaps in his understanding. But he was also sure what he had found out he'd keep to himself – for now. Somehow sharing information on a relatively small island could put friends and family in danger, he suspected. And that, for the time being, meant his family as well. He sensed that being too free with information might put his mom in greater jeopardy.

**

Representative Masato Hamilton knew that his dad had kept a detailed journal of his time on Cheju, and even published an edited version. The mention of a Professor Kang by Dr. Kim rang a bell. He found the journal passage he was looking for.

Masato pondered this entry, and came to understand that so much in Asia was driven by intense relationships. Perhaps as he sought to contribute to freeing his mother, he could keep this in mind.

***

Alex Masato Hamilton was a newly elected member of Hawaii's State House of Representatives. Elected from a tough urban district bordering the H-1 Freeway on Oahu, he ran on ideas of reform of the process. Hamilton had worked as legislative staff in the Public Access Room, and had successfully obtained funding for a local nonprofit that ran after school clubs promoting international understanding and support for poor villages in the Third World.

His name was Alex, but his Japanese American mother preferred his middle name, Masato, and it stuck. For all his friends in school, and later in his young professional life, it was always Masato, or Masa. He grew up in a family of well-educated progressive politics and service. His father, Bill Hamilton, had been a Peace Corps Volunteer in Korea in the 1970s. His mother, Eiko, was an accomplished researcher with multi-lingual language skills, who taught him that it may not be enough just to speak English well. If you wanted to understand and contribute, you needed to train your brain to think in different cultural ways.

Masato Hamilton was a member of a group of newly minted reformers that were swept into office following a major scandal that sent five Hawaii Senators to prison. Their collective platform was to frame a Bill of Rights for Citizens who came before the legislature. Respect for all, no bullshit, even distribution of power within, early availability of public testimony, more sunshine, and no backroom decisions to virtually eliminate the public government positions of employees who did not agree to do their bidding – these were some of the so-called *Democracy Culture* civil reforms they embraced. Hamilton knew it would take several sessions before the more powerful legislators accepted any changes to business as usual.

Because he was not yet a committee chair, when the legislature scheduled its yearly five-day recess, Hamilton took the opportunity to book a flight to Cheju. He didn't tell anyone, especially his father. He already had a pretty good idea of who he might try to meet in a short visit. He had, unbeknownst to his parents, found his father's Peace Corps journals in an old cardboard box.

It is rare to have an insight into your young parents, let alone their daily ups and downs in adapting to a very strange and foreign daily life far from Hawaii. Among the papers were initial letters his dad had written to kick start a Hawaii-Cheju Sister State Relationship. Most of such arrangements were merely ego boosting junkets where petty politicians pretended they were big shot foreign ambassadors. Lots of trips. Lots of big elaborate feasts. A tour here or there.

But for Cheju and Hawaii, both took the Sister State arrangement seriously. There were major conferences on planning, economic development, education, and tourism. Some were in Cheju, and some were in Hawaii. More than one governor was involved, on both sides. Over the years, at twenty- or thirty-year anniversaries, new leaders would re-affirm and re-sign vague documents pledging continued good will, friendship and collaboration.

Intertwined in related documents were connections between the University of Hawaii and Cheju National University. There were special connections among Hawaii counties and their planners, along with private planning firms that were paid to assist Cheju in its steep climb out of a poor to a thriving and growing modern economy.

Along the way, according to his father's journals and post Peace Corps correspondence, it was originally very rare for Cheju government workers or teachers to have the money or the permission to fly to Hawaii. But later, looking through the official Hamilton Library archives, a fairly large group of Cheju English teachers did visit Hawaii, a few of whom had actually been co-teachers with his father.

He'd begin there. He'd try to find and connect with and talk with some of these senior retired officials for any clues as to what was going on and why his family had gotten sucked into an actual kidnapping.

**

The aging professor Kim Ki-won was obviously frail. His wheelchair was his main way of getting around the senior center in Cheju. Yet it was obvious his mind was sharp and his English still very polished. He had taught English in a high school, then college, and was for a time the English Language Supervisor for the Island. Multiple trips to the U.S. and even a year in New Zealand had honed his linguistic skills.

"Thank you for seeing me, Professor. I really appreciate your time."

"I remember your father. He was so full of energy. He organized an entire re-write of a TESOL book for college students one summer. An older colleague, now long passed, Professor Kang, was his main booster. Kang made your father a kind of unofficial representative of the other Peace Corps people. That was fine with them because most did not really care about being involved in the educational politics of the day. They were focused on teaching, and were much better in speaking Korean than your father, to be candid. But you did not come all this way to wax nostalgia, eh?"

"What I wanted to talk about was, well, not English or Peace Corps, but some more recent controversies on Cheju. Specifically, the proposal to build a casino here in Cheju City. I wanted to know if you knew anything about who owned or controlled land around it. And especially, how or why, if at all, this could be connected to my family."

Kim, leaned forward, and whispered, "Let's go out on the balcony, where the breeze will cover up our chat." Masato respectfully wheeled Professor Kim through the sliding doors onto the balcony of his private apartment where the Cheju breeze was a barrier to any wannabe eavesdroppers.

"You can't tell anyone your source, agree? Good. Look, you may be probing into what you folks call a can of worms. I grew up on this Island, and my great grandfather was a minor official. This was during the early days of the Japanese occupation of Korea. All officials had to make the hard decision of whether to at least pretend to cooperate with the Japanese officials sent here to strut around the streets and try to tell us what to do. It was a bad time, and we don't really like to talk about it."

"Take your time. Rest assured our conversation is totally confidential. I'm just after basic information."

"This was also a time when many Cheju families were forced to move to the mainland, as their usual occupations or even land were essentially stolen. But I digress."

"No, please. Keep going. This is relevant."

"What was going on was that the emerging new economy in the 30s depended on freeing up city properties to make way for new business. But after the war, a lot of Japanese ownership reverted to the government by default, because no one really knew who originally had the rights to the land. When Japan knew the war was lost, they burned a lot of documents. But, and this is our way of resisting, we made copies of older land ownership deeds. The Japanese were, if anything, pack rats for documentation, mindless documentation if you ask me. You know, to this day, lots of Korean government institutions, schools even, keep lots of records of minor and major importance but they really don't know why. They just do, out of habit, I suppose. There are warehouses in Shin Cheju, the new part of the city up the mountain a bit, filled with documents that no one reads, or wants to read, but just can't throw away. Is this helpful? Boring, huh"

"Candidly, you know my dad was here in the Peace Corps in the 70s, and I know you met him at that time. We kind of suspected that somewhere in our distant past there was a Hamilton relative connected to Cheju. Recently, we've found information and documents to support those possibilities. I'm talking Choson Dynasty and probably before. You see, my father's family came from Europe, and were involved in centuries old shipping and trading. We don't know for sure, but I suspect we may even go back so far as to have distant relatives here. Sailors came and got shipwrecked. They fraternized with locals. Who knows, children distantly related to Europeans may have been brought up here."

"Well, you certainly have a creative imagination. The interesting thing is that Cheju was at the crossroads of lots of Asian and European travelers. I suppose if you did extensive DNA tests of today's population you'd find evidence of Chinese, Japanese, Mongol, and pure Korean families. I'm not sure why this matters. Modern is modern. Old is old. What can you do with that information other than appreciate the mixture that is what we call Asian?"

"This is really helpful. One final question, and then I'll let you go. Is it at all possible that somewhere there would be reliable records about ownership of lands, especially those who are at the center of controversy today?"

"I'll tell you what. I'll give you a name. You can't reveal your source, promise? OK. Well early Europeans were very diligent about keeping records. At Cheju University, there is another old guy like me, who is in charge of a small section of their library. If anyone has a handle on where I think you are going with this, it would be him. Here's his name on this piece of paper. Do not, I repeat, do not tell him where you got this. We used to be friends but after the recent reports and reactions to exposure of the 1948 tragic conflicts in Cheju, well, let's just say we don't talk much anymore."

"Thank you, professor. I really appreciate your time and all the information you've given me. With your permission, I'll try to keep in touch. May I email you in the future? Oh, thank you."

Masato was beginning to get a fuller picture of the history of the Island, and the waves of control and political influence over time. In his next visit, he hoped to fill in more gaps in his understanding. But he was also sure what he had found out he'd keep to himself – for now. Somehow sharing information on a relatively small island could put friends and family in danger, he suspected. And that, for the time being, meant his family as well. He sensed that being too free with information might put his mom in greater jeopardy.

**

Representative Masato Hamilton knew that his dad had kept a detailed journal of his time on Cheju, and even published an edited version. The mention of a Professor Kang by Dr. Kim rang a bell. He found the journal passage he was looking for.

Masato pondered this entry, and came to understand that so much in Asia was driven by intense relationships. Perhaps as he sought to contribute to freeing his mother, he could keep this in mind.

***

Chapter 11. The Spy and the Redhead

The leather jacket seemed a bit bulky, and pretentious for his obvious age, he thought to himself. The local Dutch baseball cap covered his head pretty well, and the blue tinted sunglasses completed his disguise, along with the high-topped leather boots. It took Bill Hamilton several hours to master control of the motor scooter. But in the end, he looked like he blended in with so many bicycles and scooters that swarmed around the city of Amsterdam.

The hotel where he wondered if his wife was held had a much older exterior than he expected. But it did have a Starburst coffee café next to the lobby, and not far away on the other side was a bar. These could provide adequate cover for his life as a spy.

What the hell am I doing? Do I really think this is going to help? Am I going to put Eiko in greater danger?

He made it a point to park his scooter near the back entrance where deliveries were made. Maybe there was something there that could provide a clue. It did not take long before he noticed two different deliveries from the back entrance as he was walking towards the coffee shop. Two Asian men carrying what looked like food were talking in what he was sure was Korean.

He pretended not to notice, but casually followed them into the lobby, and waited to see on what floor the elevator stopped. *Hmmm. Tenth floor. Almost the top.*

A hotel employee approached him and asked in Dutch if he was lost? Could he help him find his party?

"Oh, I heard there was a nice piano bar on the top floor. Is that true? Do you know if it is open?"

The hotel worker gave him a very obvious once overlook, as if to say: *What are you doing in a high-class hotel like this?*

"Were you planning on meeting a guest of our hotel?"

"I do have a meeting here tomorrow and I wanted to make sure I was not late."

"If you give me your party's name, I can ensure you make your appointment," answered the Bell Captain, obviously challenging Hamilton's legitimacy of even being in the upscale hotel at all.

"No need. I'll call my friend to confirm." Bill immediately walked out the front door and didn't look back.

Hamilton hatched another plan. He'd change into a normal business suit and head for the tenth floor. Maybe he could find out if Eiko was there.

In his new, normal, formal business attire, hair slicked down with gel, he exited the tenth-floor elevator. He positioned himself to see the main hallway with all the doors to the rooms. He waited. After five minutes, an

Asian man exited the elevator and headed down the hall. Hamilton pretended he was waiting for a car going in the other direction. He noted that the man went to the end of the hall and entered the last door on the left. He waited. He walked down far enough to see the number of the room: 1012.

Being cautious, he retreated to the elevators, went down to the lobby and out to the street, where he hailed a cab. In the hotel where he was staying, he went to the front desk and said he would like to send a dozen red tulips to Room 1012 of the Wilford. The note should read, Best Wishes on your special day. Willie.

Bill knew this was a double message, if Eiko were there and if she saw it at all. Of course, the Willie she'd know. The tulips were a bonus. When they had first arrived in Amsterdam, they'd signed up for a tour of a tulip farm, for which the Dutch were famous. But there was a screw up. Eiko got on the bus early, but Bill lagged behind getting a last-minute coffee at a fast-food kiosk near the bus departure curb. He looked up and watched the bus with his wife drive off without him. After she returned, it became an ongoing dig on how he had missed the tulip run. After that, he hated the very mention of tulips. *She would recognize the clue*, he hoped.

Eiko's Korean monitor in her room was a bit perplexed. *How did anyone know she was there? Were the cops getting closer? No, if they knew they'd beat down the door. So who? Why? Was there a leak back in Cheju? Did someone get sloppy? Talked too much at a bar? But none of these possibilities would explain why anyone would know Eiko was there.*

Hamilton had his hotel bell captain call the Wilford and ask if the flowers had been delivered and if there were any messages from the room. At this point Eiko's monitor of the day was in a near panic. He called his contact in Cheju City. The advice was to wait for further directions.

Through a convoluted communications protocol, word on the status of operations was sent back to Ko. But Ko was not available. He had been arrested by the local prosecutor. Efforts by Pu to get in touch were unsuccessful, and caused concern, especially because of his frail physical condition, getting weaker by the day, in her view.

**

The translator in Amsterdam was well paid. He located the pertinent sections of the ancient diary, and determined that a member of Hamel's stranded crew did not leave Cheju or Korea with the main group. He was ill, and they left him in the hands of a nearby village. The diary records a regret that he was left behind. They had no idea if he survived his illness.

**

The call came to the known contact to the Shinsong alumni group, who forwarded it to the TCH Steering Committee. It was not good news. As best as anyone could determine, Ko Tae-jung was taken into custody in the middle of the night. He complained he needed certain medications, but the police refused. He was apparently interrogated for three days. He died without giving up any information on the protests.

Pu was devastated. Ko had been one of the earliest leaders to inspire and organize coalitions to protest the rumored Cheju City casino. His daily blog kept everyone ginned up for action at the drop of a hat. He was their guru. His name alone could raise substantial donations. He could trace his Cheju lineage back centuries. It would be hard to replace such a leader.

Pu convened the de facto Stop TCH steering committee of the coalition. It was a small group of five who had the need to know about the Amsterdam operation. Pu emphasized they were not criminals. It was a political act. They meant no harm to this woman Eiko Hamilton.

There had been considerable, heated debate. Ko had insisted there were safeguards to ensure the woman would be comfortable, not terrorized, and respected.

The paid translator of the diary reinforced a strong suspicion that there was a potential link between a stranded Dutch sailor and his likely descendants. The key was finding evidence of a wife and children.

Their own research was that there was an oblique reference to red headed children in the village of Pyoson, also on the southern coast of Cheju. A small *sodang*, a village classical Chinese school in Pyoson run by a literati purge loser exiled to Cheju, had old records of graduates of the school, including reference to a redhead who graduated, and ultimately became a minor official on the island. If this were credible, such a position would most likely guarantee having a local wife, and even mistresses that could also have offspring. In addition, Pyoson was known to be one of the villages with a high number of Mongol horse breeders in the nearby grassy hills.

Pu said, "Ok, we may have been exposed in Amsterdam, and I'm not sure how long we can string this out for any meaningful documents. We have possibilities, speculations, wishful thinking about this one guy who was left behind. But records of this specific individual seem to have disappeared. It may be that he managed to find his way back to Holland.

We've been fortunate to manipulate Bill Hamilton to do some of our research, with mixed results. Before we give up in Europe, let's see if we can find any evidence that this sailor stayed or returned."

***

Chapter 12. Family Ties

Hamilton's burner phone rang. A link led to a voice message.

Mr. Hamilton. As you can see, we operated in good faith. We returned the book you were given custody of. If you assist us in this next task, you may be closer to seeing your wife released. Your assignment is to find out if in the 17th century there is any record of a once stranded sailor on Cheju, whose last name was De Groot, ever returned to Europe. Do not share this request with the police. If you return to your hotel bell desk, you will find the original diary that was borrowed.

The name in the voice mail struck an unexpected chord. In the narrative of his family heritage through Descendents.com, there was reference to a woman whose family name was DeGroot.

Bakker had given the diary back to Hamilton so that he could get credit for its return. He had not heard from Bakker in two days, so he made his way back to the original Museum where they got the book. He took the diary with him, hoping to establish some goodwill, and to ask about another small search of their archives.

The curator was elated to receive the diary, apparently no worse for wear. He was happy to do the research on the De Groot name.

He was in luck. An official passenger manifest record listed a De Groot who was a passenger on a Dutch East India ship that docked in Holland three years after Henrik Hamel returned. The ship's log also records a young woman and a child from Cheju on the same trip. De Groot apparently settled in Amsterdam and had several offspring. A brief outline of ancestral descendants showed a daughter who apparently married into the Hammelldon family.

Wow. I wonder if this woman links me and my family to the original sailors stranded on Cheju?

He called the number listed in the last message from the kidnappers.

"Mr. Hamilton. What have you learned?"

He told the obviously voice-altered speaker what he learned. There was what seemed like a long pause.

Tomorrow at 10 am go to the Rijksmuseum. In the men's room on the first floor, the last stall on the right, taped to the inside door will be further instructions.

Bill was tempted to call Bakker. But he remembered what his son had said about the possibility of police causing a dangerous assault to catch kidnappers. He could barely sleep that night and was up at the crack of dawn. He walked. He went out to breakfast. And finally made his way by trolly to the Rijksmuseum, famous for its Renaissance artists, especially its collection of Rembrandts.

He went to the restroom, and sure enough found the note. There was also a small envelop with a key, the kind you might use for a handcuff. In front of the campus with two museums, there was a park. The note said go to the last green bench in the park. He ran to the bench. There was a small figure in a hoodie slumped over the arm of the bench. He ran up.

It was Eiko, handcuffed to the bench. He quickly unlocked the cuffs. Eiko appeared to have been partially drugged.

"Eiko. It's me. You are free, Eiko!"

She slowly, sleepily opened her eyes and they embraced. They stood there holding each other whispering to each other for ten minutes. He helped her off to a cab stand and they took it back to his hotel.

Off to the left a Korean with a high-power camera took a number of pictures to prove that the wife had been safely returned to her family with no visible harm.

Then Bill called his son, and all had a good international cry.

***

Chapter 13. Can AI Help?

Back in Hawaii, Masato decided to use the power of the Internet to see if he could fill in the gaps. He turned to a new Artificial Intelligence application that was circulating especially in Japan. It was called GagakuTyme, and specialized in searching historical Japanese, Korean and Chinese sources to create research pieces. The questionable iffy part of using it was that once you signed up, it used facial recognition (FR) to log in. Apparently, this was a major trend in Asia, where FR was permeating a wide range of digital transactions. He paused, wondering if it could be used to steal personal information. But in the end, *what the heck, this is 2023. May as well go all in.*

His first request was for 10,000 words on the history of T'amna in the mid-15th century, the time when the Kwan-dok-jong was built.

What came up was a total gobbldegook of Chinese characters, mutilated romanizations of Korean sources, Japanese scholarship on Korea during their 35 years of Japanese colonial rule over Korea, and, surprisingly, official records of meetings with Korean emissaries paying homage to the court in Beijing.

Can AI Help?

The product was mostly an incoherent pasting together of research, obscure records from Japanese visitors to the Mongol court, official communications from a local official, a *Moksa* in Cheju, and misinformation. Most of it was in challenging languages that he could not possibly understand.

But a few nuggets stood out. First, this local Mo*ksa*, an influential Island governor of the time, as part of his "gifts" to the Chinese court, ceded 25 acres in the center of Cheju to the Chinese, who at the time were ruled by the Ming. The Ming were overthrown by the Qing, who came from the far north of Korea and shared a long history with the Mongols. Qing concubines and even an occasional queen, had roots in the far north. The Qing were very close to descendants of the Mongul ruler, Kublai Khan. This inter-tribal marriage tradition was also part of many arrangements with Korean envoys and Korean royals in subsequent dynasties.

There was no indication of just where these 25 acres were, but for Masato it triggered a direction for future probes. Cheju ownership to Ming and Qing owners. *Maybe this was a clue to look into*, he thought.

At the same time, looking in those papers he found from his father's Peace Corps days, which were stored in his attic, Masato kept running across some old correspondence between his father and a prominent Cheju personage that went off to Seoul, became a scholar, but also a trusted advisor to two future liberal Korean Presidents. His expertise was especially in international relations and North Korea. His family roots on Cheju included ownership of five acres of tangerine groves. He consistently promoted Cheju as a brand for an Island of Peace and a meeting place for international Summits for world leaders. These were meant to engage many of the movers and shakers of Cheju politics.

Ch'in Jung-in had apparently met Masato's father during Peace Corps days, when he was still a student at a prominent Seoul university. Masato remembered a nice coffee table book on the Book of Tao with mystical black and white photos to highlight each section of Lao Tse's wisdom. It was always on the bookshelf and had a personal note from Ch'in. He seemed to be a driving force on the Cheju side to promote the Cheju Hawaii sister state conferences.

I wonder if I can find him. I wonder if he would be of help in this? he thought. *Perhaps an email to that Seoul university, as he seemed to be listed as emeritus faculty.*

**

"Listen Bill, I think we should cut the ties to your insurance job and move back to Hilo. I'm not comfortable here anymore. I don't feel safe, and I don't have any idea why they kidnapped me," said Eiko wiping a tear from her eyes. *It was not like her to be emotional*, he thought.

"Maybe you're right. After all we are not spring chickens anymore. And I admit that my back and right knee are sore most of the time. I've got high blood pressure and have trouble sleeping through the night."

"And you know Masato's son is two years old and I want to have time to be a proper grandma, you know? This is our job to support them. Screw Amsterdam!" She laughed.

"Yeah, I hear you. I don't disagree. It will take a little time for me to officially resign and secure my pension from the company. If you want to go back early that's ok with me. Let me talk to the boss."

**

The hacker now had a mug shot. His annual and lucrative contract with the so-called Sogwip'o Development Consortia Trust (SDCT) sought to identify any potential threats, including people, to their plans for developments and especially casinos. So-called Facial Recognition, or FR, was not the secure application that AI outfits claimed. If you went to an airport, chances are something was recording your Face, especially in Asia. Same with a bank. ATMs. Any government application for any license. Passports for sure. Personal information was leaking all over the place. The hacker passed the picture on to his benefactor. He identified Masato Hamilton as a person of interest who may be a potential threat or impediment to SDCT's interests.

**

"Dear Mr. Hamilton. I saw your inquiry to my university office. I would be happy to correspond with you. I have fond memories of your father. I visit my family home in Cheju frequently. In the future, it would be wonderful if we had a chance to meet. Sincerely, Ch'in Jung-in

**

Text from Hyun P'il-song to Sorabong friends.

Our excellent tech contractor has identified someone that we may be concerned with. He is apparently an elected official in Hawaii, whose father lived on

Cheju in the 70s. We suspect the father, a Mr. William Hamilton, who is an insurance agent in Amsterdam, may be communicating with the protesters, and those affiliated with that communist Ko. Both Hamilton and his son seem to be showing up suspiciously in peripheral Google searches that mention casinos in Cheju. Let's keep a look out for any further involvement of this family. Hyun.

***

Chapter 14. Connecting some imaginary dots

Pu Kyung-ok was at the white board in a meeting with the steering committee. There were notes and scribbles, and arrows connecting all sides of the board.

"Here's what we know or suspect. At the beginning of the 15th century, when the Choson Dynasty was just starting, Cheju was sending regular delegations to Beijing, bearing gifts, to sweeten their relationship with China. Ming was a new Chinese regime, established not so many years before our Choson. For literally hundreds of years, descendants of the Cheju rulers and especially during Mongol times in the 1200s and 1300s not only went to China, but the Koreans took Mongol queens! Mingle mingle mingle. This practice continued during the Ming Dynasty, and later during the Manchu Ch'ing Dynasty which began in 1636."

"Ch'ing began 17 years before Hendrick Hamel was shipwrecked on Cheju. He actually stayed for 13 years, so, to some extent, we don't need to be so focused on members of his crew who might have stayed on if we want to connect this group of Dutch sailors to having some longer term roots or descendants on

Cheju. Hamel wrote a famous book: <u>Journal and a Description of the Kingdom of Korea, 1653-1666.</u> That book actually helps us to connect the historical dots."

"In Cheju City, the Kwan-dok-jong Hall was supposedly built in 1443, or the 30th year of King Sejong's reign. That's nearly 200 years before Hamel. Back in Beijing, from a delegation representing Sejong, there is a record of a gift of some 25 acres to the Ming Emperor, somewhere in Cheju City. That Hall we are talking about was designated National Treasure No. 322 in 1963."

"Wait, I'm confused," said one of the committee members. "Are we talking about the 15th century, or the 13th century, or the 17th century, or what?"

"Perhaps all of the above," answered Pu. "There was this governor, called a Moksa, back when the Hall was built. He apparently owned all those lands in that section of the city. He donated land for the Hall. But we don't really know if he donated just the plot for the Hall or a larger parcel. We do know that much later, and we are not sure about the details, but at the same time, a whole slew of official administrative government buildings were built as the Choson rulers expanded their official footprint on Cheju, and as losers in the Literati clashes in Seoul were exiled to Cheju. Those ancient buildings were burned to the ground by the Japanese, but in the last few years Cheju reconstructed them as a visitor oriented authentic museum and theme park for Choson Korea, much like some of the prominent palaces in Seoul."

"Wouldn't the ownership of all those lands have gone to the government?"

"Usually, that would be the case. But then we have this 25 acre gift to the Ming. What did the Ming do with it? Well, lots of Chinese and Korean properties were just flat out stolen by the Japanese. They burned down a lot of wonderful historic buildings. But somehow, they left this Hall intact. Somewhere there may be a record by the Japanese historians as to any old documents for lands they took over. We need to remember that as much as we loath what they did to our country, the Japanese were terrific scholars. They learned Classical Chinese, and Korean. I guess it was part of their belief that for the future Korea would be just another Prefecture like Kyushu. Consequently, they wanted to document all this for the Emperor."

"If they gave land to China, how do we connect that ownership, if we knew where it was, to this day and age?"

"Good question. I'm still struggling with all this. But here's another story that would be very interesting were it true. Let's suppose that the lands behind our Hall were not part of the gift. Maybe that is a red herring. Irrelevant. What if that Moksa kept ownership. And what if that Moksa had a family connection with the Cheju villagers of many years past. And what if some of those Dutch sailors, shall we say, mingled in a meaningful way with Cheju families while still in Korea. You know those records of red headed kids in Pyoson? And that Moksa was actually a distant relative of a Dutch sailor. And that Dutch sailor's descendants were completely intermingled with our people and actual ownership, from the Moksa on down, rested with any living relative that could prove he or she was a direct descendent?"

"Thus, our interest in that old Dutch diary?"

"Bingo. That diary, when we paid for it to be translated, had a reference to one of those sailors. One named DeGroot. Apparently, or possibly, even though Hamel left Korea after 13 years, which is a hell of a long time to intermingle, that DeGoot did not return to Holland right away. But later he did go back and started a family in Holland. That family could be, theoretically, connected to later immigrants to America. Dutch immigrants. Maybe they changed their names a bit to sound more American. Maybe a Hamel became a Hamelldon, or a Hamilton. Maybe this guy whose wife started making that connection in Amsterdam stumbled on a possible connection, through the family tree, of somebody who might possibly have, and this is a stretch, a legitimate claim to that land behind the Hall? A DeGroot of the past."

Her younger cousin chimed in. "Pu, you really have an active imagination. Wishful thinking would be a mild way of describing this wild scenario."

"Yes, I know. Not all the dots are there to connect. But, here's the deal. What if we can get enough people to believe it is a possibility. What if we create doubt. With doubt comes delay, our friend. I recently went to a court hearing where these ancient and fantastic speculations were actually put into briefs by a highly paid attorney for the casino developer. It may even be the ultimate irony if the developers made the case for our Dutch ownership hopes."

***

Chapter 15. Pack it Up... Wrap it Up

Inspector Bakker paced back and forth, almost beside himself. Seated across from him were Eiko and William Hamilton. They were the victims of breaking and entering their apartment, destruction of personal property, and kidnapping. He had no answers as to who did this. Eiko Hamilton had already been debriefed in great detail, but he wanted to hear it from her one more time.

He again re-read the transcript of one of the first interviews:

"I'm sorry Inspector, but I don't recognize any of the pictures as being those men who took me," said Eiko. *"All I know and remember is when I came home and flicked on the lights someone immediately covered my mouth and nose with a strong-smelling cloth. Next thing I knew, I was sitting on the floor with my hands behind my back tied with cable ties, and a bag over my head."*

"Do you recall anything about your captors, such as their speech. Did you hear them talk at all?"

"Nothing. I was yanked up and two strong people grabbed my arms and practically lifted me off my feet. I knew I was walked out the door, down a corridor, and on to an elevator. When we exited the building, they must have brought a car right up to the front because I was immediately shoved into the back seat."

"Was the seat anything you can recall, such a fabric or a plastic cover?"

"I'm not sure. I was very upset and disoriented. Maybe cloth."

"Do you remember how long the car ride was?"

"It seems to go on and on. Maybe at least 30 minutes. I do remember hearing a siren like an ambulance, but not just one, at least two, maybe passing a hospital but I could not be sure. But you are missing a basic question: How did I know the name of the hotel?"

"OK. How?)

"When I went to the bathroom, I opened a cabinet under the sink. I found a small thin box with a bar of soap. The box read Complements of the Wilford Hotel."

"Other than the driver, do you have any sense of how many were in the car?"

"There was someone in the back seat with me, I'm sure. And I heard the front passenger door close so maybe someone was there, so at least three, I think. But something I did notice. It was the smell of spicy food. Specifically, the smell of kimchee."

"No one said anything?"

"Once. The driver asked a question in Dutch. Seemed to be a native speaker."

Pack it Up... Wrap it Up

"Inspector, Eiko has had a long day. Could we continue this tomorrow?" asked Bill.

"Just a little more. It's important. Mrs. Hamilton, you mentioned that once you were put into a new hotel room, your handlers always wore facial masks and baseball hats in your presence?"

"That's right. I want to be clear. I was not abused. They were very kind. They mostly spoke English to me, but with a specific accent. At first, I thought it was Japanese, but later I believe their accents were Korean. And occasionally they spoke to each other in Korean. They thought I could not understand them, but I actually do understand some, mostly from watching those Korean soap operas."

"This is very helpful. Anything else?"

"That driver who spoke Dutch. At one time he showed up with takeout lunch, as I recognized his voice. Oddly, the Korean spoke to him and asked if he got the book? The driver said yes in Dutch. So, he understood both Korean and Dutch."

**

Bill Hamilton looked at the bookcase he'd need to empty and pack up when he left, filled with some of the books he just could not have done without while living in Europe. His favorites included serious essays on the major historical movements, from hunting and gathering, to agriculture to the industrial age and now the information age. Each major global megatrend was driven by new technologies and sources of energy. They still provided useful perspectives and lenses that he felt everyone should embrace. He could never toss them.

The insurance manuals he dumped immediately.

He had also brought with him a few of his favorite Asian history texts, some that were about Chinese philosophy, others on the persistence of the small collaborative associations called *kye* in Korean. Nostalgia from his days studying Korean history in the 1970s.

He'd written a major MA thesis on premodern Korean decision making. All that material was eclipsed years ago as more and more sources were translated from the formal Chinese to Korean and also into English. *I missed my chance to make a mark*, he mused.

It would take several weeks even after he handed in his letter of resignation, and moved psychologically into that new identity: retired. He'd never really thought about how emotional this would be. His entire life was driven by meaningful work. Whatever he learned seemed important to preparing him for future tasks. But now, on the brink of ending his professional life, *who the heck WAS Bill Hamilton?* He knew what was coming. *Gradually, my colleagues and contacts who were still working would stop answering my calls or emails. Forget about advice he knew they just had to have. They would not be seeking the wisdom of the quickly disappearing, fading memory of that old guy who used to have that corner office.*

He emailed his friend Ted with what he thought was a quite witty remark: *I've lost the directions to the on ramp to the highway of relevance.*

Eiko had less trouble thinking about packing up and leaving Amsterdam. It was more than the recent trauma of being held hostage by strangers. It was a gnawing understanding that her remaining years could and should be spent in her real home, Hawaii.

She was also getting tired of the Amsterdam police interviewing her over and over in search of small clues that might lead to arrests. But she did not tell them everything.

"Bill, I didn't want to share this with Bakker, but I really did recognize a distinct Korean dialect different from what you might hear in Seoul." She told him about some of the vocabulary and the ends of sentences. Bill immediately recognized Cheju *saturi*, or dialect. Not *hessimnida*, but *hessuda*.

He was dumfounded. It was bad enough to try to understand why any Koreans would have done this to them, but if they were from Cheju....unbelievable. Why? It was so many years since he'd been back there. During the 1980s and 90s he went to attend Sister State events, but most of those ties were just distant courtesy invitations. He was not sure he wanted to tell Bakker this. Not until he digested it, understood it, poked around and did his own minor investigation. One thing was for sure. After they moved back to Hilo with all their stuff, he needed to visit Cheju again.

He kept mulling over the unlikely possibility that somehow distant Dutch ancestors had co-mingled with Cheju people.

He would not need a fancy excuse to return to Korea. For years the Korean government had been graciously inviting former Peace Corps Volunteers back to thank them for their service. They gave them briefings on modern Korea, and escorted them back to the cities or villages or schools where they served. Later, during the height of Covid, Korea sent them all a care package gift with beautiful hand-made crafts and many high-quality facial masks.

DON'T MESS WITH T'AMNA
**

Pu Kyung-ok and three others met their friends at the Cheju International Airport. The flight was directly from Hong Kong.

"That was a long haul from Europe back here," said Pu. It was a party of four. Three Koreans and one European. They were quickly shuffled into a van that sped out of range of any security cameras.

On their way to the newer expansion of the city, up the mountain to what is now known as Shin (new) Cheju, Pu turned from her front passenger seat and spoke to those in the back in Cheju dialect.

"I just want you all to know that our coalition is in awe of how you pulled it off. I mean, to handle the woman with kid gloves, documenting her safety and health to all, and mostly successfully keeping your hotel a secret. And Daniel, you were really a perfect *Sven*. I'm guessing that the Amsterdam cop Bakker will never figure it out."

"Thank you. But then there was the tulips delivery. Do we know who found out, and how?"

"We have no idea," admitted Pu. "But it seems to point to Eiko's husband. Somehow, maybe in the way she recorded the video to the husband there was a message?"

"We are at least happy to get back in time for Ko's funeral. What a loss", said one of the men.

"The important thing is that we were able to nudge Hamilton into unwittingly helping us get some crucial documents from those archives. We think we may be getting closer to putting together an impressive narrative for our cause," said Pu. "Now you guys need to disappear for a while. I recommend spending some time in Sydney or Osaka."

**

RING. "Hey Dad, don't know if you saw it, but I sent you an email with links to two recent news articles on Cheju. They are from this Oakland paper that has a Seoul branch. One on a demonstration, the other on a quirky court case. I think you ought to look at them. Candidly, its possible that they are somehow tangentially related to what you experienced with mom." He didn't bother to mention his recent private trip to Cheju.

"OK, I'll look at them. Seems like a quick scan indicates a reporter has been sent down from Seoul to dig deeper into this casino business."

He kept special memorabilia related to his family in his desk, and especially his son Masato. He was so proud of his growing maturity into a future leader. One item he had kept and often re-read because it was a pretty good guide for ethnical, thoughtful and progressive politics.

This particular one-pager Masato created when he initially started his campaign for the State House, and he apparently used it to raise funds. He wrote:

" POLITICAL PHILOSOPHY

I. Situation:

    a. Hawaii & the mainland U.S. are in a mid-life crisis: like a person aged 35-40, on a career track, successful, but gradually must lower his or her dreams. Asks Now

What? Beginning to really worry about economic security.

b. Our generation feels this. The much-touted 1954 struggle is over in Hawaii. Most groups now relatively middle class. The torch has been passed. Now What? Wanting to make a difference like our parents did, but don't know what or how.

II. NEED FOR A POLITICAL PHILSOPHY

a. No one can make a contribution alone. You need a working group.

b. No group can hope to work effectively without a basic agreement to a consistent set of principles, a political philosophy.

c. Without knowledge of where we fundamentally agree or disagree, we tend to make unfounded assumptions about each other. This leads to disappointments, misunderstandings, feuds. Like the current Congressional feud. Loyalties & values betrayed.

d. Philosophy is not an abstract & irrelevant academic exercise. It is the exploration of ideas which guide our everyday lives. Cannot be left to the University. Ought to be a part of every person's thought process.

e. Philosophy cannot be derived by individual meditation, or the loyal following of a leader. Must be developed slowly, thoughtfully, in a group. Need the courage to be open and to offer ideas which might be criticized. Few people have the opportunity or the inclination to sit down with their friends and expose themselves to such a process. But if we desire to make a difference, we should be willing to make that sacrifice.

f. Our parents' generation is at a disadvantage. They cut their political teeth when issues were large and clear: Viet Nam & Civil Rights. They came out of that with a basic set of values. But those values were not necessarily always consistent, and they did not always provide a guide for the future. The issues have changed, and now we need to reexamine our values to find what principles they can be based on.

g. Many Ideas Need Clarification:

   (1) Needs v. Wants. What is the line between equal opportunity and equal results? How can we identify the threshold? Can we develop some criteria or rule of thumb to tell the difference? Are our obligations the same for human needs (a limited number) and human wants/desires (an unlimited number)?

   (2) What is human nature? What assumptions do we make about each other? What assumptions do we make about political and economic behavior?

   (3) What is political virtue? What is unethical?

   (4) What do we mean by: TRUST, RESPECT, LOYALTY, SINCERITY? What are the limits of each? How much deviation should be tolerated? How long should unacceptable behavior be punished? Is vengeance justifiable? When?

   (5) What are our personal, group, state & global obligations?

   (6) What contributions could Hawaii make to its people, to the US, to the WEST? The poor? How do we fit into the big picture?

   (7) What ideals will inspire us, and our followers in the future?"

Bill wondered, when he got back to Hawaii, what he could do to fit into his own son's thoughtful world of change. *And then there was this connection to ancient Cheju that Eiko found.*

***

Chapter 16. The Victor Writes The History

"May it please the court, we would like to call Professor Ahn No-oon to the stand," declared attorney Ku Ga-yun. Her voice was just a little less confident, in that for her, a 38-year-old lawyer was arguing the biggest case of her career, and she knew this was, as she shared with a good friend from Pusan, *A Big F'ing Deal.* She was originally from Pusan, and her family was once a prominent Kyongju clan that held sway during the latter half of the Choson Dynasty. Her father was an aristocrat, a *yangban*, and her mother a distant relative of a queen. She always strived to live up to the expectations of her family. Her brother went to med school. She went to law school.

She nervously swept her shoulder length hair back over her ear with a finger as she looked down on her notes and took a deep breath. She scribbled a note in the margin, as much to remember something as to burn off a tiny bit of nervous energy.

"Professor, have you studied the behavior of the Japanese colonialists when they pulled out of Korea after World War II?"

Ahn shifted in his seat. Although he was used to giving lectures in classes and before interested groups, he knew this was different. He'd put on his new suit that his wife insisted he wear, along with the stripped blue tie. He let her cut his hair a bit the night before.

"I am familiar with some of the recent scholarship on that. Dr. Keiji Kawamoto did some excellent work on that period. He wrote a well-regarded book which included a special chapter on Cheju. There is also an aging scholar emeritus from Cheju National University, Dr. Kang Ki-sook. I believe he used to curate a small archive on this topic that is kept there."

"Based on your knowledge and experience, would you agree that a great number of important documents, especially land use deeds, may have been destroyed at that time?"

"I think that is true. Let me rephrase. I *know* that is true. However, one way in which Koreans rebelled was that they secretly copied many records and kept them hidden. This would include land use documents that showed how the Japanese essentially took over parcels that belonged to native Cheju owners, including farmers, and former *Moksa*, or governors. Of course, the practice of granting ownership to family, friends, or colleagues hundreds of years ago would be part of that."

"Can you explain further, please?" asked Ku, making another note on a legal yellow pad, and not looking up.

"Let's say when the Koryo Dynasty fell and the new Yi clan took over, as a reward for siding with the new Choson rulers certain lands were granted to those who chose wisely. Early Choson records of course were created to essentially wipe out a loser's reputation and story and replace it with the winner. It is more than a cliché that history is written by the victors. So, if we go back to the 15th and 16th centuries, we begin to find new names and owners of valuable parcels throughout the Island. When a new King and a new clique took over in Seoul, and losers were exiled to Cheju, you find a lot of that. And continuing this practice, when Japan took over Korea in 1910, they again took land and gave it out to their perceived friends. They used land to bribe Koreans to collaborate with them."

"To summarize, if I may, genuine ownership of any parcel, such as the disputed lands in Molsulp'o, could, possibly, revert back to ownership grants literally hundreds of years?"

"I'm not an expert in a specific land use situation, but yes, I think it what you just postulated would be one reasonable view. I would add that before the land reforms laws of 1950, some 3 percent of the Korean and Japanese landowners controlled 64 percent of the agricultural lands. Most Korean farmers were tenant farmers. Those reforms dramatically reversed this. So you can see the essential theft of ownership before those reforms. "

"Thank you, no further questions."

**

Hyun P'il-song, concerned for the future power of his Sarabong Gang, sat with his attorney and two large assistants in the middle of the court room public benches. He occasionally whispered thoughts or questions to the lawyer.

"Do you think she is doing a good job? Are we winning?"

"It's too soon to tell," answered the lawyer. "As I said, this is a tricky case in terms of how it affects your interests in Cheju City. If the court takes the side of the government, that could be written in a way that kind of negates older claims. If the court goes with the Sogwip'o casino corporation, that might or might not be good for us. A casino win helps all casinos, but the land use ownership is a double-edged sword."

**

Pu Kyung-ok and K.C. Sohn were sitting together in the back of the courtroom. Earlier, they actually found a reason to have breakfast together and to share what each was looking for in the mid-morning hearing. Sohn preferred a mild tofu stew, even for breakfast. Pu tried to interest him in having what was once a popular morning jolt, called morning coffee. This was hot coffee with a raw egg mixed into it. Both were getting comfortable with each other. And both were not sure if they wanted to continue along this path.

"You see those four men up on the right side?" asked Pu. "The man in the blue suit is Hyun P'il-song. He's one of the major leaders in the Sarabong Gang, a major investor and promoter of the Cheju City casino."

"Does he know who you are?"

"Unfortunately, he and his local mafia keep track of everyone who protests and resists. We know sometimes their thugs follow us in cars, just to intimidate. Our sources tell us he may have been involved in the murder of the Vice Governor, and the recent police murder of our leader Ko."

"What? You have proof?"

"Look, even if you think you have proof, it is useless if no one will believe you or take you seriously. Or if someone has been paid off. Don't try to make a news story out of it. It will just get people in trouble. Just be aware that they are a dangerous clan to challenge. Anyone, and I mean anyone, even you Mr. big shot reporter, could be risking more than you think."

"I thought your group wanted as much PR as you could get. That would be a major story. Would get attention, you know?"

Pu shook her head. "OK K.C., I'm going to go out on a limb and ask a favor. Please don't wade into those waters without checking with me first, and, even more, if I ask you to keep it under your hat for a while please do."

K.C. looked at the sincerity of Pu's face. It was a face he was growing to like all too much, he feared. "OK. I promise. But I'm going to report on this court case and the other issues relating to casinos as I see fit."

They sat and listened as the government cross examined Professor Ahn. Nothing was revealed. None of his testimony was seriously challenged. The court recessed until 2 pm.

***

Chapter 17. The Dutch Don't Give Up on Request

Inspector Bakker sat at the table with his special investigations team. He knew he was a small cog in a large system that consisted of the National Police Corps and ten regional units. There are police officers, and 23,000 peace officers who have the power and responsibility to detain suspects and make arrests. There is a First Police Commissioner, a Chief Commissioner, A Commissioner, Chief Inspectors, Inspectors, and Sergeants. Bakker was an Inspector. Lots of higher ups to report to. And lots of pressure to make them look good.

Bakker, in a meeting with his Sergeants, desperately wanted to step out for another cigarette but that would need to wait. This kidnapping case was something that could not be swept under the rug and forgotten. The local papers and TV stations had gotten wind of it. Foreign nationals were victims. This was fodder for any politician seeking to discredit the existing government. They were all watching the large TV screen at the end of the room.

Emily DeGroot was "running" for mayor of Amsterdam at the age of fifty, in other words, she was asking and agitating for the National government to appoint her as Mayor, as is the law in the Netherlands.

The Mayor becomes the chair of a specially elected 45 member City Council, and member of a Council of Mayors and Aldermen in the city. That council is elected directly by the people. Power is distributed among a whole range of individuals, offices, and entities.

Within these complex layers of democracy, political rivals must learn to maneuver and gain influence among a maze of relationships and institutions. DeGroot had long been a rival of the current appointed mayor. A scandal in the current City Hall government, even if it was down the chain of command in a criminal case, was just what she needed to convince the higher authorities to oust the incumbent and appoint her.

"Clearly, the current mayor has not created a safe environment for our residents and visitors alike," she stated to the media.

DeGroot's Dutch heritage went way back. A once prominent and powerful family name, it had clearly lost its importance, respect and luster over the years. DeGroots who sought election to the City Council in the past were once guaranteed victory. No longer.

She was middle aged, with her hair pulled back and dark rimmed glasses. She wore a pants suit with a jacket and a man's necktie. Her intent was to project an image that said: *Don't underestimate this woman, she knows what she's doing and means business. And don't forget the heritage of the DeGroots.*

"The police department with its many chiefs and inspectors and peace officers is incompetent. They let the perpetrators of this serious crime slip right through their fingers even after supposedly posting resources at every turn. This so-called Inspector Bakker was manipulated into chasing down valuable sources at museums as if he was working for THEM, not US. I demand the City Council begin an immediate investigation as to why we as a proud city must suffer this embarrassing humiliation."

"Turn it off," demanded Bakker to his assistant. "We can't let this distract us. Forget about the politics. Just focus on the task of solving these crimes. Let's go over again what we know and don't know. I've asked our Tech guru, Liam Visser, to look at our information, and to review what we might know or not. Liam?"

"We have been collecting as much video footage from hotels, traffic cameras, and other sources as we can on short notice. Because two incidents of this story occurred near our art museums, their overhead security footage was helpful."

"Go ahead Liam, we are all ears."

"OK. We detected the same black SUV vehicle outside the hotel where Mrs. Hamilton was held, as well as within 25 yards of the Van Gogh Museum. This was rented by a Dutch citizen named Luuk De Jong. Here is a fuzzy picture of him. You can see he is about 6 feet tall, and slender. But we suspect this may be an alias. Luuk returned the vehicle to the airport and was seen walking towards the terminal. Some of you may have heard about the recent growth in Facial Recognition technology. We are beginning to deploy this at our airport and various train stations. We picked up an image of our friend Luuk and three Asian men heading towards the gates at Air India."

"Through a cooperative security agreement with New Delhi, we are able to share certain categories of passenger information. We have learned that Luuk and three Koreans named Lee, Park, and Shim, boarded the same plane with Luuk. The flight was to Mumbai. At that point we are not certain, but a similar group appears to have boarded another aircraft run out of Thailand on its way to Hong Kong. At that point, we lost track of them. However, we are suspecting that a follow up from Hong Kong to Korea's Inchon might be fruitful."

"Question. How reliable is this new Facial Recognition technology. Could it be wrongfully ID-ing someone?"

Liam tried not to appear too frustrated at the ignorance of his co-workers. "Some aspects might, but for purely identifying the same face in two locations its pretty good. I'd say 75% accurate."

Bakker was scribbling notes and looked up. "So, at this point, we are pretty sure some of the kidnappers were Koreans, but we already knew this from interviews with the Hamilton woman. And we now know, probably, they are already back in Korea, along with the European who fooled us with his Sven routine. Do we know, looking backward, when or how they entered our country?"

"They were pretty smart about it," answered Liam. "Apparently each member of this gang or whatever they are, first appeared at a transportation hub on different days, and spread over a ten-day period. This was well planned in advance."

"OK, this is useful. Now let's turn to the victims themselves, both the husband and wife. The husband has been working insurance for several years, after transferring from their London office, but before that actually grew up in Hawaii!"

Almost on cue, all the group looked out the window at the cold rainy weather and did not need to say a word, for they all were thinking how nice it would be on a beach in Hawaii.

"So, Gerritt has been in touch with the Korean Embassy and has a report."

"Yes, so we were able to track the passports of Korean nationals entering the country during this time frame. It is interesting that the three Koreans already identified list their home as Cheju Island Korea. We are currently working with the Embassy to confirm their identities. We of course have their passport names, but we are not certain these are accurate. If they are sophisticated, they could have been using aliases and doctored passports. However, we are very confident by comparing this with the Facial Recognition data that these men are the same group that flew out of Inchon Airport in Korea on the same day a month ago, all on different air carriers, and all in different directions."

**

Amsterdam Mayor Willem van der Berg did not wait long after getting a briefing from Bakker. He was appointed just three years ago and was anxious to show those who appointed him they'd made a good choice. Fairly young, at age 41, his family made its mark in retail sales. He spoke from the inside the spacious Citizens Hall of the Royal Palace of Amsterdam, built in the 17th century. Being able to pontificate from this iconic building was one major perk for a mayor. Although appointed, it was expected that a mayor would be the face and the voice of the city on major issues. In spite of the miserable weather, a large group of reporters had shown up, seeking a response to the harsh accusations of Emily DeGroot.

"Thank you for coming. I appreciate your efforts on this rainy day, but my remarks could not wait. It appears that the recently reported kidnapping of an American woman was done as a targeted attack by foreign nationals. Specifically, criminal elements of the Republic of Korea. We are currently looking into whether or not there is any connection between those who entered our city with evil intent, and Korean elements who make up what we have come to call Koreatown."

"Do we have suspects? Have you made arrests?"

"We are still in the early stages of this investigation. However, our police department has brought in several individuals of Korean descent for questioning. They are known to be associated with several gambling dens, and may also be implicated in drugs. Of course, we don't want to cast aspersions on law abiding immigrants, but we would be foolish to ignore certain cultural loyalties that could have provided safe haven for the kidnappers."

"Do you believe the kidnappers are still in the city?"

"They may be, and we are looking into this. But it is also possible that they have left the country, on their way to Korea. In any case, we call on all our citizens to be vigilant in keeping eyes and ears open for any hint of similar activities between so-called local Asians and suspicious talk. I can tell you that our hardworking police department has been busy interviewing many individuals who may have come in contact with Asians who appear to behave suspiciously. We have contracts with helpful citizens who are bilingual, and who could blend in and listen in the likely places for any loose lips."

"Are the Chinese involved too?"

"At this time, we have no hard information that links Chinese immigrants to this crime, but should it turn up we will report this to the public immediately. Thank you for coming. We will notify your organizations if we schedule another briefing in the near future. However, I would stress that our local police and our National Government Investigators are working closely together to hone in on the sources of this international incident. I am told that our Prime Minister has been in contact with the President of Korea to express our concerns and to ask for full cooperation on their end."

**

Bakker was more upset by the Mayor's press conference than that of DeGroot's. Why were so many politicians so anxious to find a scapegoat right under their noses. Paranoia goes with frustration goes with anger. And now, almost predictably, he'd have to handle a spate of hate crimes targeting Koreans, Chinese, and probably their growing Thai community as well.

He was not looking forward to it, but his aide had been contacted by Emily DeGoot, who wanted to meet, discretely. *After trashing me in the press, you've got to be kidding*, he thought.

**

"I hope you don't mind this modest pastry shop, but it's kind of out of the way and mostly private," she said. "I want you to know, right from the start, it's not personal.

It's just politics, and holding you officials accountable in the eyes of the public."

Bakker stared at her without a hint of an expression. "What is it you want?"

"As you know, I want to be the next appointee for mayor. But I want to be up and up regarding a very strange connection to your Korean case. Three years ago, my ex-husband, we were still together, gave me the gift of a search of my family's ancestor roots. The kind that combines an historical family tree, and even DNA."

"Ms. DeGroot. I'm a busy man, Is there a point to this?"

"A couple of hundred years ago an ancestor was on the crew of a Dutch trading ship in Asia. He was shipwrecked and it took nearly 20 years to make his way home, along with a woman and child. My DNA shows a small but significant percentage of Asian blood. You'll never guess where he lived until he returned. It was Cheju Island, Korea. There's more. In tracing this connection forward, it may be that I am very distantly related to your William Hamilton."

Bakker starred at her in disbelief. "WHAT?"

"I know. This is strange and amazing."

"Why are you telling ME this, if I might ask?"

"I want to be prepared should this information leak and I am somehow accused of hiding information from the public, the police, and the national government. I certainly am not going to bring it up, but frankly, for purely political aims, I want to be able to say, to prove, that I informed you people. Whether this has any impact on an investigation I don't know. I have made no effort whatsoever to contact this Hamilton guy. As far as he knows, there is no connection between our campaign, or myself. But you've got to know that I came forward." She brought her cell phone up from her lap and showed she'd recorded their conversation.

Bakker paused to collect his thoughts. Then spoke: "Ms. DeGroot, we appreciate you informing us of this distant connection to the victim. It is highly unlikely that it will have any relationship to our investigation. However, rest assured, we will include this in our overall analysis and ultimate solving of this crime. Now if you'll excuse me." He stood abruptly and left the shop. DeGroot smiled to herself.

***

Chapter 18. Keep Those Old Documents

Oakland Asia Times – Seoul Edition
K.C. Sohn reporting from Cheju Island, Korea

A Stunning Court Decision

This reporter has been following a case in the local court in Sogwip'o City, Cheju Island, between the city and a powerful development company, The Sogwip'o Development Group (SDG), over ownership of a parcel of land on which SDG is planning to build a controversial casino. After a three-day hearing during which voluminous documentation was submitted, witness testimony was heard, and oral arguments were made, and following submission of written briefs, Judge Yoo Chung-hee issued a surprising and potentially far-reaching decision in:

The People of Cheju vs The Sogwip'o Development Group (SDG) RE Dispute Over Clear Title to Parcel 34-990, Molsulp'o Township

The Self-Governing Province of Cheju had argued that it had become the legal owner of the parcels upon the departure of Japan in 1945, when governments all over Korea essentially "took back" what was allegedly stolen. However, it did not submit documentation to support the claim of ownership. Cheju also argued that it had always exercised full control and decision-making over the parcel continuously with no public objection, therefore evidencing its claim of ownership.

In opposing Cheju's claim, SDG's attorney, Ku Ga-yun, had submitted a collection of historical documents and academic research that supported the existence of a 13th Century grant of ownership of the parcel in Molsulp'o from a representative of the Koryo Dynasty (935 - 1392) to a local magistrate. Attorney Ku had produced copies of Chinese government reports from official Dynastic records, as well as peer-reviewed academic Chinese and Japanese scholarship, repeatedly referencing the transfer as fact. Other records included lists of properties not formally transferred to Cheju following the end of the Japanese colonial occupation in 1945.

Judge Yoo found that the the Cheju government failed to submit any documents or other evidence to assert ownership or to credibly challenge this land grant in the 13th century. The petition by the magistrate in 1919, and the absence of the parcel on the list of properties transferred to Cheju in 1945, implied tacit agreement to the validity of the ownership claim by the magistrate or, at minimum, a waiver of any objections to the claims. Judge Yoo further found that any activities Cheju had taken to manage the parcel had only been done on a caretaker basis until the true owner could be identified. The Judge found that title of the parcel did not rest in the hands of Cheju Government but in the heirs of the Magistrate from the 13th century grant.

In his 125-page final decision, worth reading if for no other reason than its rich historical narrative on the history of Cheju, the ownership of the parcels in question was granted to SDG.

The winning attorney for SDG spoke briefly with this reporter after the decision was announced.

"Were you surprised at the decision?"

Grinning with tears running down her cheeks, Ku Ga-yun was nearly speechless. "I am so relieved. I am grateful that the judge studied our thorough research and listened with an open mind to our arguments."

"I suppose you are going to celebrate this victory?"

Well, there is a nice makkoli house I wanted to try that has great marinated pork kalbi. Then I'll return to Pusan, and maybe take a leisurely trip to a Korean temple, like Heinsa.

The Cheju government declined to comment.

**

"Well, I guess the powerful casino lobby wins again," said K.C.

"Yeah, they usually do win. Money is power. Money is credibility. Money and the promise of jobs are hard to compete with. But have you read the decision?"

"I skimmed it, but you know, it's over hundred pages and pretty dense. Does your coalition have a formal response?"

"Not yet. Maybe never. But this could work in our favor for other places. Maybe Udo. And maybe even right in Cheju City behind the Kwandokjong. Consider this. What if we were able to find a nongovernmental owner to that land. We could cite this case. Maybe. Remember, we are protesting the action of the Cheju City government in granting a permit for the T'amna Casino and Hotel. This decision means just because the government claims it owns the land, doesn't mean the court will agree."

"Well, that seems a stretch."

"Come-on. Let's get a bus back to the city."

**

"What the hell just happened?" demanded Hyun. "Did we win, or did we sort of lose?"

Hyun's attorney was reluctant to be the bearer of lukewarm news. "Well, as co-investors in the SDG Molsup'o Casino, you will eventually win. It will get built, and you will profit. But that decision raises questions about Udo and Cheju City. It remains to be seen if either of those cases would be directly impacted by this decision because future claimants probably will not have the same level of historical documentation over time that could trump the Cheju city claim. But if they did, well, that's another story."

"So, who is our opposition in Cheju City?" demanded Hyun.

"Probably none. But we are looking into what might have happened back when that original *moksa* granted land for the Hall in the 15th century. His heirs, if they could still be found, might still have a claim to the land behind it."

"Look, I've told you before, we are not going to let anything or anyone get in the way of our Cheju City development. We are going to be millionaires in the first two years after that is built. We will have essential control over Cheju government with our connections and jobs. So, we are going to do what we can. Understand?

"Well, let's hope so. But you should know that there is a formal nonprofit group that is planning to file suit over the TCH. And, here's the not so good news. The judge who will likely preside is non other than Judge Yoo Chung-Hee!"

**

Two Weeks Later…

The police cars and sirens and yellow tape were out in force. It was a typically warm and balmy Cheju night. This was not the first-time local police had visited this site for a major crime. Just below a fashionable raw fish restaurant, a body was found in the near shore waters off Dragon Head Rock. He was identified as judge Yoo Chung-hee.

Chapter 19. The Power of A Will

Eiko Hamilton was worried about her husband Bill. He had been a proud professional all his life, and now, sooner than expected, he would set that life aside and retire. He tossed and turned at night more lately. Everything was telling him, as he said, *You Are An Old Man.*

She looked in the mirror and saw a short, white-haired Japanese American with slight pouches under her eyes. When she met Bill, she was young, with long black tresses, and a bright sparkle in her eyes. Bill was just finishing graduate work in history and was fresh from several years as a Peace Corps Volunteer on Cheju Island, Korea. He was so proud of his experiences. He even read his journals aloud to her.

Neither Eiko nor Bill wore glasses then. Now her rimless reading specs were often mounted on the top of her head. Sometimes she went through the house looking for them only to discover their perch. She used to be a competitive high school swimmer and fairly athletic. Bill was mostly bald in the back of his head, and even his moustache was beginning to turn white.

Bill was clearly stressed and agitated over the realization that his European Dutch ancestry, long taken for granted as nice to know but not that relevant, was somehow oozing its way back into his identify and life.

She was hoping that by digging into his European heritage maybe she could provide a new interest for him. They were both shocked at the DNA showing some Korean and Mongolian sourced chromosomes. And now, unbelievably, that heritage could be the reason somebody thought it would be worth kidnapping her to put pressure on him. *Find this diary. Translate it. Do it for these Koreans! What did they hope to gain?*

She got some clarification when having a private WhosApp video chat with her son, Masato.

"What? You went to Cheju Island on your own? And you didn't tell us?" she asked.

"Yeah. I didn't want to upset anyone. But what I found was interesting. There is this whole intense conflict over a plan to build a massive and obnoxious casino in the center of Cheju City right behind a Choson Dynasty building. There have been some rowdy demonstrations over it, and an Oakland Newspaper with a Seoul Office was covering the story. I think I sent links to those to both of you. One reason not to talk about it was that perhaps in conjunction with the issue a Vice Governor and an activist have been, well, murdered."

"You're kidding? Yes, your dad was intrigued but still we can't figure out what it has to do with us. The only thing that comes to mind is that someone thinks dad's heritage could connect him with ownership of the land planned for the casino."

**

Eiko was having her favorite latte in a café near their condo. She was making lists, she always made lists, of the many mini tasks involved in packing up and moving back to Hawaii. Suddenly, there was a woman staring down at her. "You are Eiko Hamiliton?"

"Well, yes, I am. Do I know you?"

"Not yet. My name is Emily DeGroot. May I join you? I think I might have some information of great interest to your family." Eiko gestured to the seat in front of her.

"I believe, Mrs. Hamilton, that my family, generations ago, has a connection to your husband's family. We are talking, actually, hundreds of years."

"Go on."

"Here is the basic story. When the Dutch sailors shipwrecked off of Cheju Island in the 1600s, there was on board a distant ancestor to me on board, a Bram DeGroot. He was with the Hendrick Hamel voyage. Hamel was stuck in Korea for some 16 years. When he finally was able to board another European ship to return to Holland, by way of Japan actually, he had to leave DeGroot behind, as he was ill. Several years later, there is a record of DeGroot returning but not alone. He brought a wife and a child from Korea. From Cheju. We believe she was part Korean and part Mongolian. The Mongols had ruled over Cheju for at least a hundred hears, and there was a lot of intermarriage. While captive, Hendrick Hamel and his surviving crew were able to communicate because a previous Dutch castaway, Jan Jansz Weltevree, was able to translate. The Korean King at the time didn't want the outside world to learn about Korea, so he told them they could never leave Cheju. But Hendrick and a few managed to escape to Japan, to the European outpost at Nagasaki, called Deshima. Eventually they made their way back to Holland.

"So, if I am leaping ahead, perhaps you are a distant relative of them, and at some point, my husband's family tree connects him also to the DeGroots?" asked Eiko.

"That's the short version. The DeGroot-Cheju child was a young boy. When he grew up, he married a first cousin of Hamel. So you've got some DeGroots and some Hamels. At the time, it was not unheard of that cousins married cousins."

"Ok, we know from the Descendents.com print outs that my husband is distantly related to both Hamel and DeGroot. And he has DNA that is a little bit Korean and Mongolian. So that would mean he is distantly related to the DeGroot son of the sailor and the Cheju woman. Did I get that right?"

"Yes. Very good. And this also means, because of my DNA, Mr. Hamilton and I are probably also related. "

"All very fascinating, I'm sure. But is there a reason you sought me out to tell me this?

"Yes. When Hamel and DeGroot returned to Holland, they brought with them some diaries and documents. It was common to grant plots of land to these foreigners to put up a house, and grow their own food. The Cheju government being very document oriented, there were official deeds to such land, to protect the occupants. My family has in its possession of what we believe was essentially a deed to land in what is now Cheju City."

"As my son would say, cool. Is there a reason to tell me this story? I'm a little skeptical because you are a stranger."

"I'm sorry, I love to tell the details. Several generations later, the Hamels created a Foundation, which exists today. It is focused on Dutch history, the family, the role of the Dutch in Asia, and other areas. These ancient deeds are part of the Hamel Foundation archives. And we believe that our family could, if it wanted to, become involved in seeking to establish current ownership of that land."

"Oh, and the connection to Bill?"

"The Foundation also has several original wills that grant to the surviving descendants of Hamil and DeGroot, including personal and real estate property. We have found that there is a Hamel family will that includes the DeGroot lineage. The Hamel will gives certain property, mostly in the Amsterdam area, ownership. It also included a provision that if there were are no Hamel direct descendants, that property goes to the original offspring of the shipwrecked DeGroot. We have consulted with lawyers, and believe me, Dutch law is unbelievably arcane and complex, that your husband and I have equal claim to two properties. One here, and one-are you ready- in Cheju City."

"Oh my. Are they valuable?"

"Well, that depends on who wants it and who could use it. I can tell you that if you folks agree to forfeit any claim to the Amsterdam parcels, I am prepared to do the same for the Cheju land."

Eiko's head was bursting with the implications. Could this be the reason she was kidnapped?

"So, Ms. DeGroot, your story isn't astounding. But I don't know very much about you. I mean, no disrespect, but how do I know this isn't some kind of scam or fraud? Can you tell me more about who you are and why I should believe you?"

For the next hour, DeGroot explained who she was, and confessed her desire to be appointed mayor, in accordance with the Dutch political system. The parcels she apparently co-owned through a will with Bill Hamilton were along the waterfront in Amsterdam, and would, she admitted, generate a huge income in the future. But her plan would be to create a homeless shelter and a business run by former orphans. Eiko took notes, and they exchanged emails. She would brief Bill on this and get back to her.

**

"Ms. Ku, my name is Pu Kyung-ok. I am a Cheju resident. I was an observer at the recent SDG case."

"Ok, Pu Kyung-ok, look. I was just doing my job. If you are going to harass me, or threaten me, I will report you to the police."

"No, no, you misunderstand. Our coalition of interested Cheju organizations would like to HIRE you."

***

Chapter 20. Welcome to Hawaii of the East

It took Inspector Bakker a week to convince his superiors that if they were to have any hope of solving the Hamilton case and bringing the criminals to justice, he would have to go to Korea. Reluctantly they approved air fare and a one week visit to Cheju Island. He would travel with one other member of his staff. He obviously did not speak Korean, so he would need to hire a translator.

An official inquiry was sent through the Embassy, and a native Cheju speaker would be waiting for them at the airport when they arrived. She was a junior bureaucrat in the Cheju Institute of International Relations. She'd been to the states for her undergraduate degree in Asian Studies at the University of Hawaii. Suh Duk-hee was a 27-year-old rising star because of her bilingual abilities, and for this she was resented by some of her less educated male co-workers. She was also a graduate of Shin-Song High School. While in Hawaii, she briefly dated a young history major, Masato Hamilton. But that did not work out when he met his future wife.

"Welcome to Cheju Island," she said in her best perky voice to the weary Dutch travelers. "I have your hotel all reserved. I'll drive you myself."

Bakker and his high-tech guru Liam Visser loaded their bags into the trunk and looked forward to a hot shower and a nap after the long flight. Suh chatted away as she drove pointing out this or that feature of the city, and she stopped briefly as the clouds blew away from the top of Mt. Halla, the extinct volcano that dominated the skyline everywhere on the Island.

"I just wanted you to get a glimpse of the mountain." She said proudly. "People are getting ready to climb it in large numbers in ten days for the azalea festival. Maybe if you have time…"

"Sorry, Ms. Suh, is it? We don't have time to be tourists. We need to try to find out about fugitives from a crime committed in our country."

"Oh, right. Yes. I received your information through our office. I've set up three meetings tomorrow with our law enforcement officials. The Facial Recognition data is already in their hands. And we also have a meeting with an archivist at Cheju National University to discuss the possible connection between Dutch sailors, and land use controversies in the City. I hope you don't think I was presumptuous by going ahead."

"No, no," said Bakker in a weary voice. "We need to move quickly. We only have one approved week."

**

After dropping off her guests at a new hotel in the Tapdong section of the city, Suh headed for her favorite restaurant where her class alumni were having their monthly get together. The unbelievably alluring smoke and aroma from the marinated pork kalbi greeted her twenty feet before she opened the sliding door to the restaurant. Her former classmates were in the back room, which easily held all twelve of them. The soju bottles were already opened by the early arrivals when she slipped off her shoes and sat at the low table with a central cooking burner in the middle.

As soon as she sat, her longtime friend Pu Kyung-ok came and sat next to her. They hugged, and poured each other a shot of soju. Pu knew about the arrivals from Amsterdam, and hoped later she and Suh could have a chat.

In Cheju, everybody knows everybody....

**

Eiko and Bill spoke to Masato as she briefed them on her meeting with DeGroot. Masato cautioned about believing such a story, and shared Eiko's suspicion that they were possibly being used or manipulated, if not outright defrauded.

"The thing to watch out for is when they ask for your personal information. Under no circumstances should you give in to this. Let her provide details that we can check out. I've already been on the Internet and it appears that this Emily is a real personality and politico in Holland. And some of her assertions seem to fit with what Wiki says."

"So, do you think the connections are logical, plausible, actionable?" asked Bill.

"I think they are worth considering but need to be solidly verified. But I admit, this is the first real breakthrough that connects some of the dots between Amsterdam and Cheju. I have an old friend, a kind of old flame, that works as a translator in Cheju. She and I were, er, friends back when I started grad school and she was an exchange student. I'll try to find her contact number or email. I think she works for the Cheju government in some capacity, but we haven't been in touch for years."

"When is the legislative session over?"

"Beginning of May. Why?"

"Look, it is almost impossible to clarify anything from Europe or even Hawaii. I propose we find a way to all go to Cheju soon. We could pretend we are tourists there to climb the mountain. Kind of undercover while we poke around. What do you say?"

"Masato, what do you think?" his mother asked.

"Well, why not? Susan can get her mom to babysit, and we can all go. If you can get to Hawaii several days early, we'll all go from here?"

"It's a plan," said Bill. I have just handed my official resignation letter in, and I think I can get my company to help arrange to send all our stuff back to Hilo. We'll have time to box it up, and sort it out, but let's all try to pull this off in the next week. OK?"

"My, aren't we characters in another Ludlum novel," said Eiko. "I'll call Air Holland right after we end this call. Masato, can you get reservations with Korean Air?"

**

The next morning four men, three Koreans and one European, boarded planes out of Cheju. One was to Osaka, Japan. Another to Hong Kong. A third, to Manilla. The fourth to Australia. Each wore a large facial covid mask, and had a hoodie to cover their heads. They were travelling with doctored passports under false names. Dark sunglasses completed their outfits. It would be nearly impossible to accurately match them with any Facial Recognition screening.

**

Hyun P'il-song was not a happy man. Initial requests to continue to engage the services of Attorney Ku, were unsuccessful. She was out of the office, and they did not know when she would return. But he had a backup. The Sogwip'o Development Group had a lot of talent. An articulate representative, Hong Dae-shik, was also an attorney. They could trust him. He was a stickler for administrative and financial detail. *We'll get him*. Besides, he wasn't sure the previous attorney fully appreciated the differences between the Molsup'o case and the Cheju City application for a building permit.

**

Six days after their initial plan, the Hamiltons boarded a plane for Cheju.

***

Chapter 21. Gambling on a Friendly Reception

The delegation of casino operators, construction executives, and Shanghai investors looked up at Song San's Ilchulbong Peak, or Sunrise Hill, the massive rocky caldera of an extinct offshoot of the eastern end of the Mt. Halla volcano. Swarms of tiny hikers could be seen making their way up the sides to peek into the abyss. It was one of Cheju's scenic hot spots. Fifty years ago there was just a small village at its foot. Now, the parking lots and buses took over acre after acre near the approach.

They opted for a leisurely yacht trip out to the small island of Udo – Cow Island, wishing to avoid the riff raff on the regular tourist ferry. "Udo was once mostly known for its Cheju diving women. Its population of less than 2,000 residents has learned to survive mostly on tourists," Hong explained.

The delegation was scoping out a potential site for a new casino. They did not expect to be met with a feisty delegation at the dock of over 100 protestors with homemade signs. SAVE UDO. NO MORE CASINOS. GO BACK TO SEOUL. RESPECT OUR ISLAND.

TURN AROUND AND GO HOME. They chanted. They shook fists in the air.

K.C. Sohn knew they were coming. He was tipped off by his new friend and lead protestor, Pu. Before their arrival he'd interviewed some of the residents. There was still a contingent of working diving women on the island, and they were the core of the resistance, as far as he could tell.

After landing their yacht, the investors quickly boarded a limo and set out for their development site. Pu said their guide for the day was the SDG attorney and slick PR man Hong Dae-shik.

She had confronted him days earlier.

"Why do you insist on ruining our island? We are already way beyond our carrying capacity. Practically every good restaurant favored by locals is overcrowded because you guys put it all on the Internet and it draws tourists like flies," she said.

Hong was not easily provoked. He'd perfected a relaxed, soft-spoken demeanor even when being harassed.

"Now Ms. Pu. That's an old Cheju name, right? The three mythical originators of all the Cheju people? Ko, Yang and Pu?"

"Don't try to smooth talk and change the subject, Hong."

"You come from a family of diving women, I'm told. You must be proud of that tradition. Was your mother a diving woman? It's so amazing how they can hold their breath so long."

"There you go again. What is amazing is how you can

avoid the real issues that the Cheju people truly care about. How you pretend that you care about us, but all you really want is large profits in the pockets of people who don't give a shit about us and live far away."

"Well, actually I grew up here and live here with my family. We are fifth generation residents. So, it's kind of unfair, I think, to be spreading such misinformation. You know, there are a lot of Cheju families that have a pretty good living in our hotels and casinos. They are not complaining. Maybe you should stop shouting long enough to understand your own people."

"You'll find out how our people really feel at the public hearing tomorrow. I advise you to take notes. You might learn something, Mr. fancy traitor Hong."

"Oh, I do look forward to that. I do hope you will attend. And bring your friends. We are anxious to describe how our casino proposal will lift the standard of living for all the families here on this wonderful garden of Eden of Udo."

Hong moved off to speak with his delegation who were a bit concerned at their reception.

"Not to worry. They are a small minority. In the end they will welcome you and the new Udo Reno of Cheju."

**

K.C. Sohn decided to wait before filing an article on the Udo informational meeting. But he did send an email to Seoul. In it he reported that of the 1,700 residents of Udo, three hundred showed up to protest the future imposition of a casino on the small island. Not a single resident spoke in favor of the proposal.

K.C. and Pu celebrated with her aunties and other diving women. The raw fish and harvests from their daily dives, sautéed in garlic and butter, were the best he ever had.

There was no need for another article by Sohn because a local paper, the Halla Inquirer, published an extensive review of the meeting, with quotes from several who testified. The Cheju Monthly also covered it, with additional research into the expected costs of building a casino, the expected profits, and the likely negative impacts on the small island.

**

Hong Dae-shik tried to explain to his clients that this was "just a passing expression of their pride, and it would fade in time. They will give up the fight eventually." *Like that never happens in the history of Cheju*, he admitted to himself. They returned to Cheju City on their yacht that night. In the coming weeks, Hong was informed that the Shanghai investor group was not yet ready to commit to Udo.

"This Pu, whatever her name is, has become a big pain in the neck," Hong told his aides. We are going to have to remove this irritation sooner or later."

***

Chapter 22. Crime and Punishment

Bakker and Visser spend two hours at the Cheju Police Station. They provided as much information as they had in the hopes that local authorities could identify and arrest the kidnappers. The police chief nodded politely, but Bakker recognized that look that cops have when they are just being polite but have no hope of finding a criminal.

The meeting took longer because Suh Duk-hee needed to translate back and forth between English and Korean, even though she suspected the meeting could have been conducted in English. The Cheju police are too proud and stubborn about insisting on speaking in their native language, she believed. Just making a point.

What they were not expecting was the revelation that there were crimes in Cheju where three murders might be mixed up in the kidnapping story. Suh also knew that one of them, the death of the protestor Ko Tae-jung, was at the hands of the police themselves. Both are wanting to blame someone, and to cover their asses, she reflected.

They parted cordially, promising to share any information that might help each other. Later, Suh phoned Pu with a short report.

**

Oakland Asia Times – Seoul Edition

K.C. Sohn reporting from Cheju Island, Korea

Island of Peace Disturbed by Violent Crimes

The sleepy and beautiful Hawaii of the East, Cheju Island, may not always be the idyllic refuge that tourists dream of. In the last year, three stunning murders have taken place with no arrests, let alone convictions.

It began with the shocking beating death of the Vice Governor, Lee Yong-ho. His body was found floating on the shoreline. To date, there are suspicions as to who might have been involved but no formal arrests. Police admit they have no strong leads, but some have blamed protestors who opposed his support for casino developments on the Island.

In fact, one of those protestors, Ko Tae-jung, was taken into custody for questioning. Tragically, after several days of interrogation, he died. Police point to an ongoing medical condition. However, some police representatives speaking off the record insist that Ko was a real suspect in the murder of the Vice Governor.

Most recently, a well-respected judge, Yoo Cheung-hee, recently ruled in favor of a proposed casino on the southern coast of the island. Yoo Chung-hee, was found drowned at the same location where the Vice Governor was found. Police site this as circumstantial evidence that the perpetrators might be the same.

This reporter has also learned that a recent kidnapping of an American woman in Amsterdam, Mrs. Eiko Hamilton, was likely perpetrated by residents of Cheju. Police are unable to link all these crimes, but there are two representatives of the Amsterdam police who have recently arrived in Cheju to investigate this apparent link. To date, there is no announcement as to whether the suspects have been identified or located.

A representative of the Cheju Governor speaking off the record suggested that all of these serious crimes tend to paint Cheju as a bit less of a favorable environment for outside investors.

A spokesperson for those peacefully protesting the building of more casinos on Cheju, Pu Kyung-ok, admitted that discouraging casino investors is one of their overall goals, but that attempts by police and others to implicate protestors in crimes they cannot solve suggests there is a level of corruption and conflicts of interest deep within the government.

Despite the wide publicity of these crimes, Cheju is expected to see over 10 million visitors this year. This is roughly the same number expected to visit Cheju's sister state, Hawaii. The Hawaii resident population is twice the size as that of Cheju.

**

After what was clearly an unproductive meeting with Cheju police, Bakker and Visser were escorted around Cheju City by Suh. She took them to the East Gate market, and then a short stroll through the aging narrow Ch'l Song Tong commercial street. They exited at the western end near the Cheju Province Post Office, and were escorted towards the prominent Choson era Pavilion, the Kwan-dok-jong.

As they stood in front of it, with Suh explaining its origin, another small group wandered up to take a look. Bakker was preoccupied with his own thoughts. He glanced off at a familiar voice. Staring at them in disbelief were Eiko and Bill Hamilton, and a younger couple.

"Hamilton?"

"Bakker?"

"Masato?"

"Duk-Hee?"

They came together and started all talking at the same time, all asking questions, all trying to process their shock and feelings. It was all a jumble of Dutch, English, and Korean. They settled on English.

Duk-Hee went up to Masato, who introduced his wife, Susan. Susan and Duk-hee briefly sized each other up, but then maturity got the better of them and they relaxed. What was then is over. This is now. We are all blessed to have found a better path. A better life, thought Suh.

The next scheduled meeting for Bakker and Visser was not until 3 pm, so they awkwardly all agreed to have lunch together, and to share why they were all there.

As they enjoyed their miso stew, something Bakker and Visser had never eaten, it was clear the one person who seemed to know something about everything was Suh Duk-hee. She explained her role as a translator, and the meeting with police. She also gave her personal view of what might have been going on with the protestors, without actually revealing her relationship with Pu. She briefed them all on what some already knew about the recent protests in Cheju City and Udo, and the ironic court case ruling in Sogwip'o.

No one at the lunch was ready to be completely open or candid about their opinions, their goals, their knowledge, their distrust, or their next steps. Liam Visser said nothing, and was focused on his cell phone searches. He looked up what he could find on Suh and Masato Hamilton. The only tidbit of information that might be relevant was the high school Suh attended.

***

Chapter 23. Wisdom From Winston

Dr. Kang Ki-sook was flattered that so many distinguished visitors wanted to meet. He'd been head of the historical Cheju archives at Cheju National University for decades. Almost no one paid any attention to him or his documents for years.

In his youth he was one of the original members of a college English language club known as the SEAL Club, which stood for the Society of Eagles and Lions. Bill Hamilton had met him many times while in the Peace Corps. His wit and charm had led the Americans to nick name him Winston, after Churchill. Winston helped so many novices in the Korean language to learn new phrases and vocabulary.

Bill remembered when Winston taught him the Korean phrase: " It would have been good if...xxx " (*xx het tu ra myun, cho ashil tend de...*) They would go to a tabang, a tea room, and all afternoon, in Korean it would be: *It would have been good if we ordered coffee; It would have been good if Kim Dae-Jung had defeated President Pak, It would have been good if that tea room girl would have agreed to go to the movies with* *me, It would have been good if we did not get so drunk last night….*on and on until that grammatical phrase would never be forgotten.

Bill and Kang embraced on seeing each other. Both had tears that spoke of their friendship, renewed after so many years. Bakker and the others were not sure they were confident about how honest or unbiased this conversation could be.

Suh explained to Kang in heavily laden Cheju dialect, almost a completely foreign language to many mainland Koreans, who each person was and why they were here, and what they needed or wanted, as far as she could tell. Bill recognized the verb endings, but still could not understand most of it.

Eiko and Susan just sat politely and sipped the barley tea that had been prepared for them. They would watch and try to glean meaning from references that might be too Cheju-centric for them at first. Masato pretended that he was just a bystander as well, notwithstanding his recent secret trip to Cheju or his research on its history.

Bakker began in English, which they all agreed was acceptable to everyone, that they needed to better understand why someone like Hamilton, with a family that originally came from Holland, would be connected, even remotely, to a current land issue in Cheju.

"If I understand your interests correctly," Kang began, "it is important to appreciate the larger context of Choson Dynasty land use in Cheju," he began, assuming a very professorial, professional tone. He was telling them he was speaking not as a long-lost friend but as an expert.

"First, you need to know that despite the many disruptions, conflicts, changes in government, rebellions and even wars, all the major players from Silla times believed in keeping detailed official records. Imitating China, which was the gold standard for official behavior, and using the lingua franca, so to speak, of most of Asia, the classical Chinese characters, Silla, Koryo, the Mongol, Choson and Japanese officials employed dedicated librarians and clerks and historians to record every debate, every decision, every change in land use and ownership. They all believed in it. It doesn't mean all those records survive, but they were once honored and kept."

"But the second thing is that when you borrow a new set of clothes, it doesn't mean you've become the person that lent them to you. When you want to show China you are an independent nation, you might use their language, their office names, their institutions, many trappings of your big brother, so to speak. But Koreans always had their own way of doing things, and what might have been a strictly vertical governance structure in Xian or Beijing, could become an egalitarian club in Korea. Are you following me?"

Kang's audience was trying to be polite, but Bakker yawned. Visser's eyelids were almost shut. Eiko and Susan found their attention shifting to the scrolls and traditional furniture in Kang's office. Bill and Masato were doing their best to pay attention to information they pretty much already knew. Suh was busy texting on her phone.

Kang looked around and read the room. "Oh, sorry. I do get carried away. Didn't mean to go into my lecture mode. Bill, it would have been good if I'd skipped to the good parts," he said in Korean. Bill chuckled and let Kang know, yes, he remembered his favorite language lesson.

Bakker asked, "Is there something more recent you can tell us?"

"At the time the Pavilion was built in the early 15th century, the local government was still honoring a gift, or perhaps a theft, of lands in Cheju City to the Mongols. Their descendants had several small vegetable plots, houses, and a Cheju pony stable in the immediate area. The Pavilion, for military training, was a gift to King Sejong. He ruled from 1418-1450, and is most noted for creating the Korean phonetic alphabet. The Mongols kept their land holdings and possible buildings including a horse stable nearby. Later, when one of the losers during King Sejo's reign, who was Sejong's son who ruled from 1455-1468, was exiled to Cheju, he tried to acquire those lands. Sejo was a brutal tyrant and created much turmoil. But there is a reference to a local government decision to reject this request. It's not a long passage, but it's there and we have no reason to believe it isn't valid. Sorting all this out is no small task."

"But here's the interesting part. That Mongol family in the 17th century had a connection with some of the shipwrecked crew from Holland. In fact, in the 19th century there were Koreans living in Cheju City that ran a small village school, called a *sodang* that were kind of famous for having red hair. By the way, there is a nice adage in Korea that goes: *Even a School House Dog will learn something in three years!*"

"So, you think some of those landowners in the 19th century were descendants from the Dutch?"

"It's plausible. Many of us in Cheju believe that. There is no other explanation for the red hair. But its complicated, sorting out who owned what, when, how, and the mixing of ethnicities."

"OK, so let's fast forward to the 21st century, shall we," said Bakker with no attempt to hide impatience.

"Yes. Well, when the Japanese took over in 1910, or really earlier, they were gaining control, they stole lots of land that they wanted. They created phony deeds for the entire center of Cheju City, including the Pavilion and the land behind it. What they didn't want they burned down. An entire administrative complex from Choson Dynasty days was lost. That has recently been rebuilt. And then when we kicked them out after World War II, the local government assumed control. Their view was that what Japan stole we shall now own. But they didn't make a big effort to find out who they stole it from."

"Dr. Kang," Bill began. "Is it possible then that we may have lost information on the Mongol side of the ownership, but that the Dutch side could still exist?" He glanced at Eiko, remembering the extraordinary meeting with Emily DeGroot. It was too soon, he believed, to reveal her information.

"That is one possibility," answered Kang. "In Cheju, this is not a completely unfamiliar situation. Recently a local court found that with an unbroken and unchallenged chain of custody documentation a private landowner was granted final ownership over the local government."

"Is there an administrative way of sorting this out?" asked Masato. They all looked at him as if to say, *Are you still here. What do you know?*

"Yes. Turns out there is a special Administrative Land Use Adjudication Office that is quasi-judicial, and holds hearings, and can decide in disputes. But you've got to understand that there are time limits for filing appeals. I made a few inquiries. The land near the Pavilion is presumed to be under the control of the government. And the government is currently considering the request to lease the land to a private developer. There is, however, a deadline. You have two weeks to file a petition to challenge government ownership. If no one comes forward, it will be the government's call as to whether to issue the lease."

Bill could not contain himself. "Dr. Kang, is it at all possible that if land were granted to a foreigner centuries ago, if they could show its validity, that the administrative office would be open to considering it? Hypothetically, of course."

"It's possible. But I caution you internal bureaucratic deadlines are taken very seriously. If such a claim were filed, you'd need to move very quickly. There is no flexibility, here."

**

Bakker and Visser met privately that night to sort out their situation. "Liam, I don't know if you can check on the accuracy of what this Kang guy was telling us. But clearly, if he is to be believed, there are interests here in Cheju that would have benefited from what went on in Amsterdam. Kidnap a wife, motivate a husband, secure an obscure document....maybe make the case that long lost Dutch sailor with an ownership deed could still make a case for a claim. If that's the case, then we need to ask ourselves who would most benefit from such a scheme?

"Yes, boss. I've been thinking about that. You know there is that Hamel Foundation that has a lot of old documents. I wonder if they could help us out on this."

"Yeah, but we need to be careful. There would surely be highly motivated interests on all sides to either validate or eliminate such a claim. Would someone willing to kidnap an innocent woman be capable of fraud or even raw violence? Remember, there were several murders down there that, who knows, could be connected. Are the beneficiaries part of a local mafia?"

***

Chapter 24. Know Your Law

Attorney Ku set up a small office in the *Hyunde Yogwan*, a small inn still operating off a narrow alley connecting to Seven Star Street. She had piles of notes and documents and newspaper clippings spread across the floor. Her desk was a foldable one-foot-high table normally used for meals. Containers from takeout meals were piled in the sink. A small refrigerator contained essentials, along with some Orion draft beer, which she favored.

Plugged into the wall was a portable printer. Two legal yellow pads were filled with scribbled notes. The deadline loomed, and she was beginning to doubt if she could pull this off. Her primary contact with the Stop TCH consortium that hired her was Pu Kyung-ok. Ku knew that Pu was deeply involved in the protests, and had been a known associate of the late rabble rouser Ko Tae-jung. *What have I gotten into?* she pondered.

The day before, Pu walked briskly to catch a cab after her initial meeting with Ku, and meet up with Sohn at his hotel. Despite the costs to the Seoul office, Sohn had persuaded his editors to extend his stay until the upcoming administrative hearing.

**

Hyun convened an emergency meeting of the Sarabong Gang. It was in his spacious penthouse office above the South Sea Bank Building at the main rotary in the City.

"Gentlemen, our attorney Hong tells us there is nothing to worry about. The likelihood of a successful claim being filed in time is nearly zero. We are here to ensure it IS zero. I for one would be very disappointed if such a claim were actually filed at all. Am I clear about this?

"Sitting at this conference table are leaders in every major sector of Cheju's economy and, yes, even government. It is obscene to think that we cannot prevail in this. It is not acceptable that we do not secure that lease and build our new T'amna Casino and Hotel. In the days to come I will reach out to each of you to learn what you, with your resources and connections, can do to make this happen. I don't need to remind you that we have a sworn oath, a bond, that cannot be broken. Together, we will make our future Hotel the future of this Island. It will make us all wealthier than we can imagine. We can't let a few crackpot radical communists get in our way."

**

No one knew she was coming. Few knew who she was, or what she looked like. Mostly. Bakker and Visser would know. Eiko and Masato made sure she would slip in unnoticed to Cheju and be invisible. The flight was from San Francisco, through Kumamoto, Japan, and on to Pusan. A tourist boat from Pusan brought her to Cheju City. When it was dark, Pu escorted her to Ku Ga-yun's yogwan.

"Did you bring the documents?" asked Ku, looking frazzled.

"Yes. Here are the printouts, and on this flash drive are the records of incorporation for the Foundation, and a chain of custody dating back to when the DeGroot's were granted certain lands."

"And the agreements with Hamilton?"

"Yes. As per our agreement, the Foundation will assert that I am the

valid owner of that property. Should it be needed, we can reveal that William Hamilton and I have equal rights that are quieted in his favor per this signed and notarized agreement. But I am hoping that the claim of the Foundation alone will be sufficient as to not reveal Hamilton's involvement."

"I will be the judge of whether we need this or not," said Ku.

"How does it look. Are we good to go?" asked DeGroot.

"You never know about these things. With Judge Yoo in formal court, I would've felt more confident. But now he is gone, and we have decided to go the administrative route rather than a full-on court case. Of course, this could be appealed, in which case we are back in court."

"Ms. DeGroot," began Pu, "I just wanted to thank you again for paying for Ms. Ku's services. It would have been a stretch for our coalition."

"My pleasure. But let's be adults here. I have a special interest. Hamilton and I are going to split our ownership and forgo any joint claims. I give you Cheju. He gives me Amsterdam."

As Pu and Emily DeGroot were leaving the inn, they were walking down Seven Star Road. It was nearly midnight. Suddenly, a motorbike sped towards them and they could see a passenger with an arm stretched out. A gun went off. Pu and DeGroot dived to the pavement. Someone came out of a small shop shouting "Hey, what's going on?" The motorbike came to a halt. Another shot. It did a U-turn, and disappeared back from where it came.

"Holy Mother of God, what is going on?" muttered DeGroot. "Ms. Pu, are you all right?"

Pu looked up and tried to stand, but she quickly collapsed. DeGroot saw the blood on the cobblestone walkway. "Help. Help."

**

Word spread quickly among Pu's associates. It was not long before K.C. Sohn got a phone call in the middle of the night. Pu had been taken to a nearby clinic recently opened where the older Shin-song High School had been located. When Sohn rushed in, he was informed that she had been initially treated for her wound and sent by ambulance up the hill to the hospital.

He was not allowed to see her in the ICU until the next afternoon. Crimes with guns were rare in Korea. Someone had the capability to smuggle weapons into Cheju, he suspected. When he was escorted to her ward and bed, there was an unknown western woman in a chair by her side.

"Who are you. Is she OK?" demanded Sohn.

"She is going to be OK, but she lost a lot of blood. I don't know you sir, but I assume you are a friend. She was shot in a serious spot in her leg where there was a major artery. A translator, I think it was a Miss Suh, was here and the doctors told me she would recover but needed several days and close observation until she could be released."

"OK, and who are you again?"

"My name is Emily DeGroot. I am a Dutch citizen. I am here on confidential business with Ms. Pu. We had a late meeting when we were attacked. And who might you be?"

"I am K. C. Sohn. I'm a reporter for the Oakland Asia Times Seoul office. I've been covering the recent protests and other issues here on Cheju. I have been working closely with Pu."

Emily could see the concern in his eyes and concluded he was sincere. Just then, Pu opened her eyes and smiled. "K.C."

"Kyung-ok. I'm here. Are you feeling better?" said Sohn.

"K.C. I'm a bit tired, and doped up too. But they say I'll be fine. K.C. did you meet Emily? Emily is helping us with our legal petition to secure ownership of the Pavilion lands. She's come all the way from Holland, can you believe? So, you two are probably a bit frazzled or tired, but not as tired as me. Why don't you go to a Starburst Coffee Shop or something and talk to each other. And Emily, maybe K.C. can help you find your way back to our attorney so she can be clued in."

**

Later, they briefly met Ku, who was very upset at the news of the shooting. She was curt with them as she had a lot of work to do, but insisted that she might need protection as well. *Someone must have followed Pu and DeGroot to my hotel room. They know where I am, or who I am.*

"Look," said Sohn. Recently I've met some of Pu's friends. I'll contact them and see if they can provide some volunteer security here."

Within an hour ten muscular diving women were surrounding the yogwan, at its entrance, and outside attorney Ku's door. No one was going to get past them. When the police arrived, everyone insisted they knew nothing about a nighttime shooting. They were just friends of the occupant.

Ku made her own phone calls. An affiliated law firm experienced in criminal law in the city was briefed by Ku. "When this is over, I want to go after the perpetrators. I want to put them in jail for a long time." A follow up with investigators of the firm went to the scene of the shooting and found spent bullet shells.

***

Chapter 25. Just In Time

Oakland Asia Times – Seoul Edition
K.C. Sohn reporting from Cheju Island, Korea

The Dutch Come To Korea...Again

It has been an unprecedented and eventful two weeks in the Self-Governing Province of Cheju. A local activist was wounded. A major casino development has been thwarted, a local police chief arrested for corruption, and a prominent Dutch politician named DeGroot, flew in to successfully claim land near the hallowed Kwandok-jong Hall in the center of Cheju City.

One month ago, if you were a gambling person, you would have bet your money on a new lease from the Cheju government to the Sogwip'o Development Group to build a 35-story super luxury casino and hotel immediately behind the Choson era pavilion. And you would have lost that bet.

In an unexpected twist of legal fate, an Amsterdam Heiress associated with the Hamel Foundation successfully petitioned the administrative land office to recognize a legitimate claim of ownership dating back centuries. Emily DeGroot is a direct descendent of a shipwrecked sailor in the 17th century, one of the crew led by Hendrick Hamel. DeGroot, through her local attorney Ku Ga-yun, was able to provide convincing documentation that her great great great great grandfather was given a deed to contested Cheju lands and that the Hamel Foundation was the legal owner today.

Following this astounding and surprising decision, DeGroot revealed that she was actually a co-heir, through a will, with an American insurance agent working in Amsterdam. That agent had a long history with Cheju.

William Henry Hamilton, III had served as an American Peace Corps Volunteer in Cheju in the 1970s. His family heritage was actually European-Dutch. It turns out that he also was related to Hendrick Hamel and the seaman DeGroot. He and the Foundation are co-heirs of the Cheju lands and parcels in the city of Amsterdam.

Emily DeGroot and William Hamilton came to a mutual agreement wherein she will own the Dutch parcel, and he will own the Cheju lands.

What will he do with it?

"I love Cheju and its people. I love the history of this city. This land deserves to be preserved to benefit and educate future generations. I am establishing a foundation that will create a park immediately behind the Kwan-dok-jong, and just beyond a museum dedicated to one of Cheju's most important communities, the Diving Women. The Museum will also have space to train future generations of diving women. This Foundation, as owner, will have as its charter a prohibition against all commercial development. Any uses of the lands in the future will need two thirds vote of its Board of Directors. The Foundation, in a separate agreement, will be managed by Cheju National University. The first chair of the Board will be Emeritus Professor Dr. Kang Ki-sook. We are very excited to be a part in preserving the pride and dignity of a special place and a special people," said Hamilton.

The casino proposal had been promoted by the influential Sarabong Gang. It's leader, Hyun Kil-do, was recently indicted for bribing a police chief to falsely arrest a protest leader, Ko T'ae-jung, who died in their custody. An ongoing investigation of this issue and potentially related crimes is ongoing.

**

Ch'in Chung-in had made the arrangements for one of the largest and most popular Cheju City restaurants, with several spacious rooms to accommodate groups. The guests for the evening were an unlikely collection of people who would never have dreamed of sharing a banquet a few short weeks before. He smoothly made his rounds to greet each, with something of interest to share with each.

Inspector Bakker and his assistant Liam Visser were there, reconciled to the fact that they did not hunt down any kidnappers and probably never would. They were in deep discussion with Emily DeGroot, who told them there would be room in her administration if she ever were appointed mayor.

The four Hamiltons, Bill, Eiko, Masato and Susan were chatting with Suh Duk-hee and Dr. Kang Ki-sook, who Bill was now referring to as Winston. They were boring

Masato, Susan and Eiko with old stories of Cheju in the 70s that sounded as if they were massively embellished.

Pusan attorney Ku Ga-yun was in deep legal conversation with the newly appointed Interim Chief of Police. All, with blushing red faces, were obviously into their second or third bottle of True Dew Soju.

The room erupted in applause as K.C. Sohn pushed Pu Kyung-ok's wheelchair through the door. He wheeled her to each of the groups for her to give her sincere thanks for helping to save her island, as she put it.

The special black pork marinated kalbi, a Cheju delicacy, was brought out in massive amounts, as were the tofu and miso stews, and plenty of fresh raw fish and shells harvested by Pu's aunties.

It was a celebration and a great relief.

Sitting together, K.C. and Pu whispered to each other.

"So, Mr. fancy Seoul reporter, I guess you'll be going up to your lavish office in Seoul, yeah?"

"Well, actually, I've persuaded my boss that we should open a special branch right here in Cheju City, and I'm going to be head of it."

Pu's lips slightly quivered, and she wiped happy tears from her eyes. She poured K. C. another shot.

***

About the Author

Jim Shon earned a degree in Music Education from Syracuse University in 1969 before serving 3 and a half years as a Peace Corps Volunteer on Jeju Island when he taught middle school English and conducted teacher workshops. Exerps from his journal were published.

In 1973 he studied Korean history at the University of Hawaii. His unpublished thesis was: The Intuitive Arena: Decision Making in Premodern Korea.

At the University of Hawaii he developed Hawaiian history for public high schools. He served in the Hawaii

State Legislature for 12 years, where he was chair of the Committees on Health and Environment.

During this time, he initiated a Sister State relationship between Jeju and Hawaii. In 1996 he was honored to become an Honorary Citizen of Jeju.

In 2001 he received a PhD focusing on Aging and community services. He later was head of Hawaii Charter Schools, and Director of the Hawaii Education Policy Center. He authored several fiction books on Hawaii as well as nonfiction including Inside The Capitol, The Unfinished Health Agenda, and A Charter School Story. He visits Jeju regularly.

www.ingramcontent.com/pod-product-compliance
Lightning Source LLC
Chambersburg PA
CBHW031154020426
42333CB00013B/653